The 400 Blows

The 400 Blows

a film by François Truffaut from a filmscript by François Truffaut and Marcel Moussy

Edited by David Denby
General Editor, Film Book Series: Robert Hughes
Grove Press, Inc., New York

Acknowledgments: Frame enlargements and other stills are printed with the kind permission of Janus Films (A. William J. Becker III and Saul Turrell), the present American distributors of the film. We also wish to thank Lucette de Givray of Les Films du Carrosse, and Helen G. Scott, who provided the poster, the production stills, and much assistance that is less apparent; Jonas Mekas provided the issues of *Cahiers*. The French dialogue was translated by David Denby; the excerpts from the original screenplay by Henry F. Mins; and Helen R. Lane translated all the supplementary material from the French. Design is by Stephanie Tevonian.

Contents

A Note on this Edition

> The most fantastic thing you could film
> is people reading. I don't see why no one's
> done it . . . The movie you'd make would
> be a lot more interesting than most of them
> are.*   —*Jean-Luc Godard*

Making books from movies (apart from noveliza-
tions) is a relatively recent enterprise. But until
everyone has inexpensive access to prints of his favorite movies and can "read" them whenever he likes,
this is one means to understand a particular film. In
these books, the origins, some of the transformations
and, by extension, the resulting structure may at least
be suggested and can be studied and discovered at
leisure.

As in all Grove Press film books—from *Hiroshima
Mon Amour* (1961) to *I Am Curious (Yellow)* (1968)
—nearly all the illustrations are frame enlargements
taken from the film itself. Because this film is in
CinemaScope and because no economically feasible
method is as yet available for adequate resolution
and quality reproduction of such images, the frame
enlargements were drawn from a "flattened" print.

As in *I Am Curious (Yellow)*, *Masculine Feminine*,
L'Avventura, *Rashomon*, and this title, the principal
text consists of a meticulous description of the significant action and a translation of the actual dialogue in the completed film rather than that of the
"final" (or original) shooting script, which often

---

*Godard said this during a *Film Quarterly* interview
(Winter 1968–1969) in the context of discussing the
mixing of genres—theatrical and cinematic.

varies greatly from the final version of the film. Because no definitive text existed at publication time for the last of Truffaut's subsequent (1966 to date) revisions, and because in any case they are not as yet incorporated into prints in American distribution, their inclusion must await later editions of this volume.

In our text of the finished film, camera position is indicated by initials after its first use: LS for long shot; MS, medium shot; MCU, medium close-up; CU, close-up; and ECU for extreme close-up. The stills keyed to the text should suggest the meaning of these terms. Camera movement is indicated by the following: *pan* (camera turning sideways while remaining fixed on its axis); *tilt* (camera moving up or down while fixed on its axis); *dolly* (camera moving toward or away from the action); and *truck* (camera on its axis moving laterally to the action—sometimes literally on a truck). We have also noted in parentheses after each shot its duration in seconds. The supplementary materials — articles, interviews, reviews, documents, etc.—may give additional clues to the mysteries and insights of this film. The *Cahiers* "collage"—a tribute to the style and the solidarity of the film-nuts (the critics, scholars, propagandists and, ultimately, the moviemakers) who launched the so-called New Wave—was assembled by the general editor. The principal text of the film itself, as well as the other supplementary material, is the work of David Denby, a recent graduate of the master's degree program in film at Stanford University. The principle has been to include information not otherwise readily available concerning the creation and the reception of this film but to leave to further study how the film relates to the director's other work and/or to film history. Our hope is that these measures in the interest of accuracy will be useful to the student of film and not obtrusive for the general reader. They may assist either to visualize the action and perhaps even to realize the director's decisions in presenting a particular scene. A final word about the film's title, *Les Quatre Cents Coups*: according to *Dictionnaire du Français Contemporain* (Larousse, Paris, 1969) this colloquial expression is defined as "to deliver one's self over to every sort of excess." To which we add: raise hell.   —R.H.

The Film

Title Sequence. The title sequence consists of a number of traveling shots of the Eiffel Tower, taken from different angles and streets; a variety of Parisian architecture appears in the foreground. The theme music continues throughout the sequence. (The credits will be found on page 156.)   (158 seconds

1 *Close-up of a schoolroom desk, seen from over the shoulder of a young boy. He is writing. He puts down his pen and pulls a pin-up picture of a girl in a bathing suit out of the desk.*

After a quick look he passes it ahead and the pic-

ture moves rapidly up one row and across three. As the camera pans we see the class: a group of perhaps forty boys, twelve or thirteen years old, anxiously keeping up the appearance of studying for their teacher, who sits at a large desk in front. (He is known to the students as "Little Quiz.") The pin-up makes its way to Antoine Doinel, a dark-haired boy in a turtleneck sweater. He draws a moustache on the picture.

LITTLE QUIZ: Doinel! Bring me what you have there.

Antoine reluctantly walks up to the teacher, a dour-looking man in a full-length coat, and hands him the picture.

LITTLE QUIZ: Ah! Very nice! Go stand in the corner!

Antoine goes to the corner and disappears behind a small blackboard which stands on an easel. He reappears momentarily on the other side of the easel holding his nose and grimacing. The class laughs.

12

LITTLE QUIZ: Quiet! Only a minute left!

CLASS: Oh!

LITTLE QUIZ: Quiet!

He moves between the rows of students. (56

2 *Medium shot. The teacher walks to the back of the classroom. The students are bent over their papers in deep concentration—except for René Bigey, who stares at the ceiling looking for inspiration.*

LITTLE QUIZ: The papers will be collected in thirty seconds.

Protests from the class.

LITTLE QUIZ: Quiet!

He walks to the front of the room, stopping to encourage a tousle-headed boy by cuffing him on the head.

LITTLE QUIZ (*looking at his watch*): Monitors get ready. I'll count to three. One . . . two . . . three . . . Collect the papers!

Student monitors spring to their feet. René gets a sudden inspiration and begins writing; the others lift their heads and slap down their pens. (34

3 *Medium close-up. René is writing furiously. Bertrand Mauricet tries to collect his paper, but René pushes him away.*

RENÉ: Collect the papers in the back!
LITTLE QUIZ (*off*): What's going on?
MAURICET: He won't give me his paper, sir.
LITTLE QUIZ (*off*): No favoritism.

Mauricet finally pulls the paper away.

RENÉ (*to Mauricet*): Brown-nose! (16

4 *MCU. The teacher stands in front of the easel, collecting papers.*

LITTLE QUIZ: Has everyone handed in his paper? You can go.

There is a general rush to the door. Antoine pops out from behind the easel.

LITTLE QUIZ (*off*): Oh, no, not you, my dear student.

Antoine stops in his tracks. Little Quiz walks past him, pointing toward the corner.

LITTLE QUIZ: Recess isn't a *right*. It's a reward!

He continues to the door, his arm pointing toward

the corner. He goes out and locks the door behind him. Antoine goes back to his corner, furious. As he passes the blackboard he throws an eraser in the air, but it is attached to the board by a string. (32

5 *Long shot from above of the schoolyard. Some students are playing games; others are involved in discussions. Two boys fight a duel with their notebooks. Another rides on his friend's back.* (4

6 *MS from above. A group of students stand talking near Little Quiz and a colleague.* (1

7 *MS from above of a group of six students. Two wrestle while another plays with a shovel. The camera pans left to several other boys who are in a pushing and shoving fight.* (12

8 *CU. Antoine, in his corner, reaches up and starts writing on the wall. We hear him reading to himself.*

ANTOINE: Here suffers poor Antoine Doinel
Unjustly punished by Little Quiz
For a pin-up that fell from heaven . . .
Between us it'll be an eye for an eye, a
tooth for a tooth.   (4

9 *MS from above. In the schoolyard, Little Quiz
breaks up a scuffle between two boys; he grabs them
by their necks and drives them out into the center of
the yard.*

LITTLE QUIZ: O.K., champions. What you need is a
referee. You'll train for three days without a recess
. . . three days of rest, that'll do you some good.
Go on, go on!   (13

10 *CU. Antoine lowers his hand and examines his
work.*   (1

11 *MS. The students rush back into the room. René
breaks away from the group and runs behind the
easel. Mauricet follows him, then sticks his head
back out.*

MAURICET: Look at this!

*Antoine pushes Mauricet away, but the damage is
done. Boys crowd in on both sides of the easel.*

LITTLE QUIZ (*off*): What's so interesting there?

*The students flee in all directions as Little Quiz goes
behind the easel. He pulls Antoine out by the scruff
of his neck and pushes him into the room. Little Quiz
digs his hands into his pockets in disgust. Antoine
hangs his head.*   (27

12 *CU. Little Quiz looks back and forth from Antoine
to the class.*

LITTLE QUIZ (*with heavy irony*): Marvelous, we have
a new Juvenal in the class! Only he can't tell the

difference between an alexandrine and blank verse.
(6

13 *CU of Antoine, from the teacher's point of view.*

LITTLE QUIZ: First: Doinel, you will conjugate for
tomorrow . . . (2

14 *CU. Little Quiz stands in front of the blackboard.*

LITTLE QUIZ (*to Antoine*): Go to your seat. (2

15 *CU. Hanging his head, Antoine walks to his place.*

LITTLE QUIZ (*off*): Take this down. In all the tenses
of the indicative, the conditional, and the subjunctive . . . (6

16 *CU of Little Quiz, hands on hips.*

LITTLE QUIZ (*to the class*): The rest of you, take out
your recitation notebooks. (*He sits at his desk,
purses his lips, and looks up at Antoine.*) (4

17 *LS. Antoine sits down and gets ready to write.*

LITTLE QUIZ (*off*): "I deface the classroom walls, and
I mistreat French prosody." (11

18 *CU. Little Quiz stands and goes to the blackboard.*

LITTLE QUIZ (*to the class*): "The Hare." (7

19 *MS of the class. In unison, heads drop and pens are taken up for the dictation.* (5

20 *CU. The teacher turns around with a show of weary contempt.*

LITTLE QUIZ: Second: Doinel, go immediately to the concierge and bring me something to erase this nonsense . . . (3

21 *CU. Antoine looks up.* (3

22 *CU. The teacher. He gives a vindictive toss of his head.*

LITTLE QUIZ: Or else, my friend, I'll make you lick them off! (*The matter closed, he turns back to the board and begins writing out "The Hare." He speaks without stopping or turning around.*) Richer, who gave you permission to change places? (11

23 *CU. Antoine slaps his pen down, gets up, and walks out, dejected. The camera pans to the tousle-headed boy on the right-hand side of the room. Little Quiz can be heard reading the lines of "The Hare" aloud as he writes them down, his voice rising and falling. The boy writes laboriously, his head bent down and bobbing as he moves his pen across the page. Suddenly dissatisfied, he rips the page out and with some difficulty turns toward the back of his notebook.*

LITTLE QUIZ (*off*): "In the season when the
bushes . . .
Flame with vermilion flowers . . ."
(25

24 CU. *Little Quiz is writing on the board, his back
to the camera.*

LITTLE QUIZ: "When the black tips . . ." (5

25 CU. *The tousle-headed boy dips his pen in the
inkpot, only to have the ink drip on the page. He
sticks his tongue out in dismay and pulls more pages
out of his notebook.* (8

26 CU. *Little Quiz is writing and reciting.*

LITTLE QUIZ: ". . . of my long ears . . ." (3

27 CU. *The boy starts to turn the page, but his
hands are by now so ink-stained that he has to tear
out more pages.*

LITTLE QUIZ (*off*): ". . . could already be seen . . .
above . . ." (11

28 CU. *Little Quiz looks rapidly from side to side as if he were searching for inspiration.*

LITTLE QUIZ: "... the still-green rye ..." (*He turns around and looks at the class to see who's working, then whips back to the board.*) (8

29 CU. *The boy is still wrestling with his notebook.*

LITTLE QUIZ (*off*): "... from which I nibble ..." (4

30 CU. *Little Quiz turns around in the middle of a phrase.*

LITTLE QUIZ: "... the tender stalks ... as I play about ..." (16

31 CU. *The boy accidentally drips still more ink on the pages. He desperately tears off the dirty pages and stuffs them under the desk.*

LITTLE QUIZ (*off*): "One day . . . comma . . . tired out . . ."

The boy lifts the notebook off the desk and is astonished at how thin it is. The camera tilts up and pans to the door as Antoine enters carrying a pan and sponge.

LITTLE QUIZ (*off*): "I was asleep . . . in my hutch."
(25

32 LS. *The classroom from the rear. Antoine walks down the right side, waves to the class, and darts up behind the teacher to make the sign of the cuckold behind his head.*

Great suppressed amusement. He darts away and goes behind the easel.

LITTLE QUIZ: "Little Margot surprised me there."

Little Quiz turns around too late to see Antoine.

LITTLE QUIZ: "I'm not the only one," eh Simonot?

SIMONOT (*popping up from his seat in the rear*): I didn't do anything, sir.

LITTLE QUIZ: Of course not. It's always someone else.
(12

33 CU. *Antoine is standing in front of the wall on which he has composed his poem. He begins scrubbing.*

LITTLE QUIZ (*off*): "Indeed, she liked me . . ." (3

34 LS *of the classroom, as in shot 32. Antoine can occasionally be seen scrubbing the corner wall behind the easel.*

LITTLE QUIZ: ". . . my affectionate little mistress."

At this line, general pandemonium breaks out. Some of the boys embrace each other in mock passion; others, in the manner of Marcel Marceau, encircle their own necks to give the appearance of a couple embracing; another throws kisses to an imaginary audience of admirers.

Little Quiz turns around and restores order with a piercing glance. He moves to his desk.

LITTLE QUIZ (*still reciting*): "How good she was,
    What care, what tenderness!
    How she hugged me on her little knees . . ."

He turns to the board and the general disorder resumes, accompanied by cooing noises.

LITTLE QUIZ: ". . . and kissed me."

Whistles and sighs. Little Quiz swings around.

LITTLE QUIZ: What imbecile whistled? (*Dead silence.*) I warn you, I will be unfair—if the guilty one doesn't confess, I'll punish one of you as an example. Right, Simonot?

SIMONOT (*popping up*): I swear it wasn't me, sir.

Little Quiz throws the chalk at him.

LITTLE QUIZ: Cowards too, eh? What a year! What a class! (43

35 CU *of Little Quiz, hands on hips.*

LITTLE QUIZ: I've known idiots before, but at least

they were polite. They stayed in their seats—in
their corners.   (4

36 CU. *Antoine, too frightened to return to his seat,
lowers his eyes during the last part of this tirade.*

LITTLE QUIZ (*off*): And you?

Antoine's head snaps up.   (4

37 CU. *Little Quiz faces Antoine.*

LITTLE QUIZ: Do you think you've cleaned it up? No,
  you've made it dirtier, my friend. Go to your seat
  and copy this recitation.   (4

38 CU. *Antoine walks off glumly.*   (1

39 LS. *The entire room from the back. Antoine walks
to his place on the left.*

LITTLE QUIZ: I pity France in ten years!

He goes to his desk and throws a book on the floor.
                                                      (5

40 MS. *The camera tilts down from the "Liberty–
Equality–Fraternity" bas-relief statuary group above*

the school entrance to the students pouring out of the door. René and Antoine come out and turn left.

RENÉ: Everyone swipes money from his parents.
ANTOINE: Yes, but it's still difficult.
RENÉ: Even Mauricet, I bet. Hey, Mauricet . . . !

They stop in front of Mauricet, who is wearing black rubber goggles.

RENÉ: Where'd you buy those fancy goggles?
MAURICET: At the Hôtel de Ville.
RENÉ: With dough swiped from your old man?

Mauricet shrugs his shoulders and walks off. They shout after him.

RENÉ: Don't tell us you didn't, you hypocrite!
ANTOINE: Bastard! It was you who squealed on me!

They turn away and walk back past the school entrance.

ANTOINE (*looking back and shouting over his shoulder*): Dirty rotten stinker!
RENÉ: Your days are numbered, Mauricet!
ANTOINE: You'll get yours, Mauricet! (34

41 LS. *The two turn right onto the Rue des Martyrs.*

ANTOINE: I'll never finish tonight.

They approach an empty bench. (14

42 CU. *They sit down.*

ANTOINE: That bastard Little Quiz.
RENÉ (*laughing*): That's his job.

ANTOINE: Before the Army gets us I'm going to sock
him one.

*They get up. Antoine passes behind the bench,
reaches across it to shake René's hand, and runs into
his house.*
Dissolve.[1] (14

---

[1] Superscript numbers refer to sections of the original
screenplay which were left out of the finished film and
which are included in this book, starting on page 159.
—Eds.

43 MCU. *Antoine, inside his parents' apartment, stokes a coal-burning heater. Music begins. He goes across the room and wipes his hands on the curtains, then pulls some money out from where it has been wedged under the top of a high sideboard.*

He counts it quickly, puts it in his pocket, and

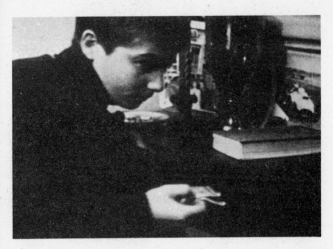

opens the door at the side of the room. (31

44 MS. *The door opens into another room. A small bed is in one corner. Antoine slips quietly into the room and sits at his mother's dressing table. A mirror is propped on the table in front of him and the full-length mirror on the back of the closed door is at his side. He brushes his hair down straight in front, then takes a sniff from a large bottle of toilet water, tries out a metal eyelash curler, and finally, tiring of the game, gets up.* (37

45 MCU. *He moves to a breakfront, takes some bowls*

from the cabinet below and begins laying them out on the table. He repeats the process with glasses and silverware. He goes briefly into the hallway, gets his briefcase, and returns to the table. He opens his notebook and lays it out flat.

ANTOINE (*writing*): "I deface the classroom walls . . ."

Someone enters the apartment. He looks up and then quickly stuffs his notebook into his briefcase. The music ends. (65

46 *MS. Mme Doinel is at the end of the hallway. She is fashionably dressed in a sealskin coat which she removes and hangs on a hook. Auto-club stickers and pennants decorate the walls of the hall and·the dining room.*

ANTOINE (*off*): Hel-lo, Ma-ma.
MME DOINEL (*curtly*): Hello.

She walks back down the hall toward the door leading into the kitchen. The camera pans back to Antoine, who takes his notebook out again.

MME DOINEL (*off*): Where's the flour?

Antoine looks up.

MME DOINEL: Why didn't you buy what I wrote down? Where did you put the list I gave you?
ANTOINE: I lost it. (26

47 *MS of the entrance to the room. Mme Doinel can be heard in the hallway.*

MME DOINEL: No wonder you get bad marks. (*She sits down just outside the room and begins removing her stockings, revealing a good pair of legs. Peremptorily:*) Bring me my slippers.

Antoine crosses the room and goes into the bedroom.

MME DOINEL: They're under my bed.

28

He stops in front of her, his eyes lowered.

MME DOINEL: And get the flour. I need it.

She grabs the slippers from his hand as he passes in front of her. He continues down the hallway.   (25

48 CU. *Mme Doinel examines her face closely in the*

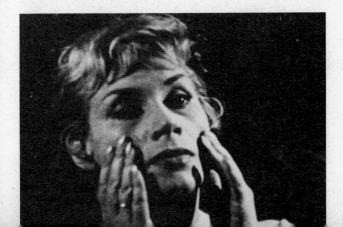

hall mirror, smoothing the creases in her skin and the bags under her eyes.[2]   (7

49 MS. *The building's stairway, looking down. Antoine and his father are coming up.*

DOINEL (*looking down at Antoine*): Always running, son?

Antoine, carrying the package of flour, rushes past Doinel and then slows down to talk.

ANTOINE: Mama bawled me out.

They turn at the landing and continue climbing.

DOINEL: I hope you're not going to make your mother cry again. You know you have to be careful with her.   (11

50 MS *of the stairway, one flight higher.*

ANTOINE (*nodding at a package in Doinel's hand*): What's that?

DOINEL: A fog-light for the car. I'll try it out at the rallye on Sunday.

Doinel dips into the flour and powders Antoine's nose. Laughing, they reach the top of the stairs and stop in front of the apartment door.   (13

51 MS of the inside hallway. Doinel and Antoine enter, the latter rather sheepishly.

DOINEL (calling into the kitchen): Look at your son . . . all floured up.

Mme Doinel comes out of the kitchen and snatches the flour from Antoine.

MME DOINEL: Believe me, you're not funny. (She goes back into the kitchen.)

DOINEL (moving down the corridor as the camera dollies back): And I thought I was.

He puts his package down. He and Antoine begin hanging up their coats as Mme Doinel comes out of the kitchen.

MME DOINEL: Give me the change.

ANTOINE: I need some money for the canteen.

MME DOINEL: Talk to your father.

Antoine gives her the change. She disappears. He and his father move toward the dining room.

DOINEL: The swallows sure fly low now . . .

Mme Doinel follows them.

ANTOINE: Papa, I need money for the canteen . . . I only need 1000 francs.*

Mme Doinel brushes by them on the way to her room.

DOINEL: Meaning you hope for 500 . . . but need only 300. (He reaches into his pocket.) Here's 100 . . . (Antoine shrugs; Doinel gives him more.) All right, 500. Anyway, your mother's paying.

Mme Doinel comes out of the bedroom.

MME DOINEL: Where are my scissors?

DOINEL (sings): Where are my scissors . . . ?

---

* Old francs. There were four hundred to the dollar at that time (1959). —Eds.

Antoine sits down, smiling. Mme Doinel, not at all amused, stands with her hands on her hips.

MME DOINEL (*to her husband*): You needn't laugh. (*Turning to Antoine.*) Don't do your homework now. We're about to eat. (*She turns and walks down the hall.*)

DOINEL (*looking at Antoine*): She's right, you know. Everything in its time and place, and (*clowning again*) the cows will be well guarded. (*As he says this he sits down and prepares to eat.*)   (54

52 *CU of Doinel and Antoine. Antoine is putting away his pen and paper.*

DOINEL (*picking up the pen*): Where's this pen from?

ANTOINE (*groping for an answer*): I traded it.

DOINEL (*frowning*): You've been trading a lot lately.
   (8

53 *MCU of Doinel and Antoine at the table, seen from above.*

DOINEL (*sniffing*): What's that? Do you smell it?

ANTOINE: It's the fish.

DOINEL: Go ask her if the dish towel is burning.

ANTOINE (*not understanding*): Why?

DOINEL (*winking as Mme Doinel comes in*): Just as a joke.

Mme Doinel puts a pot down on the table and sits, her back to the camera. The camera moves into a CU of Antoine, who holds his soup plate up to his father.
Dissolve.   (32

54 *CU. Antoine traces the outline of his fingers on the table with his knife. The camera moves behind Doinel as Antoine rises.*

DOINEL (*to Mme Doinel*): Your cousin telephoned. His wife's expecting again.

Antoine begins clearing the table. Doinel folds his napkin elaborately. (13

55 *CU of Mme Doinel, smoking.*

MME DOINEL: The fourth in three years! Like rabbits . . . disgusting. (2

56 *CU. Antoine passes behind his father on the way to the kitchen.*

DOINEL: Apropos, what are we going to do about the kid's vacation? (4

57 *CU of Mme Doinel.*

MME DOINEL: Well, there's always camp.
DOINEL (*off*): At that age, they have more fun being with one another.
MME DOINEL: We still have eight months to think about it. (5

58 *CU of Doinel.*

DOINEL: You can't plan too early for vacations.
Dissolve. (3

59 *MS. Antoine and Doinel are unrolling a long banner in the corridor.*

DOINEL: Don't pull it too much there . . . She's a beauty, isn't she?
ANTOINE (*reading*): "The Lion Club."
Mme Doinel comes out of the kitchen, ducks under the banner, and walks to Doinel.

MME DOINEL: What's this?

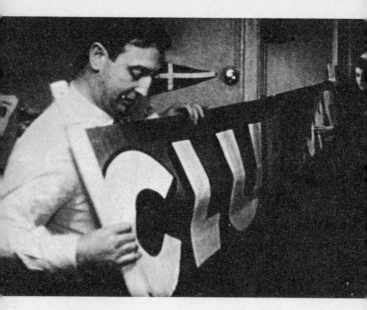

DOINEL: Be careful. (*He rolls up the banner.*) Where would you prefer to drive Sunday? The auto club asked me to plan Sunday's route.

MME DOINEL (*looking down at her knitting*): I'm going to rest Sunday.

Antoine has rolled up his end of the banner. He stands in front of his parents during this discussion.

MME DOINEL (*snappishly*): I'm going to spend the day with my friend Huguette.

DOINEL: I'll look great. Some organizer!

MME DOINEL: Every morning I have housework and in the afternoons . . .

DOINEL (*interrupting*): In the afternoon you practice the "touch" system (*typing with his forefinger in the air*) on your typewriter or on someone else's.

Mme Doinel turns abruptly to Antoine.

MME DOINEL: Antoine, why aren't you in bed?

Antoine puts something down on a table and goes into the hallway, closing the door as he says his goodnights.

ANTOINE: 'Night, papa, ma . . .

His mother shuts the door on him rudely.

MME DOINEL (*looking furiously at Doinel*): You and your jokes! (41

60 *MCU of Antoine in his alcove in the hallway. He moves a chair and begins to unroll his sleeping bag on the floor. His parents are arguing in the next room.*

DOINEL (*off*): The day you can take a joke . . .

MME DOINEL (*off*): Exactly! You waste your time on drivel. (*She opens the door and looks in.*) Antoine, don't forget the garbage . . . and turn off your light when you go to bed.

She closes the door and Antoine goes into the kitchen, the camera panning with him, and pulls the garbage out of a cabinet under the sink. Meanwhile the quarrel continues.

DOINEL (*off*): The rallyes mean contacts. When the club makes me vice-president . . .

MME DOINEL (*off*): But you'll never be vice-president . . . They just need you to jog along at your little job. (17

61 *MS of the hallway. Antoine comes out of the kitchen and slips out the door.*

DOINEL (*off*): In other words, I'm good for nothing? (6

62 *MCU. Antoine leaves the apartment and goes down the stairs. A radio is playing patriotic songs. He has apparently heard this argument before.*

DOINEL (*off*): Why'd you marry me, then? (4

63 *MS from below. Antoine rounds the corner of the stairway and continues down the stairs.* (5

64 *MCU. Antoine hurries on down the stairs and empties the garbage into a can. The automatic light goes out and it is pitch black. When the light comes on, Antoine is pushing the button with one hand and holding the garbage with the other.*

He puts the lid back on the can and goes up the stairs.
Fade out. (26

65 *Fade in to MS of Mme Doinel as she enters the hallway in a nightgown. She rouses Antoine.*

MME DOINEL: Hurry, it's late. We didn't hear the alarm.

Antoine quickly rubs the sleep out of his eyes and stands up, still in the sleeping bag. He pulls the sleeping bag down like a pair of pants, steps out of it, sits on his bed, and pulls his pants on. He gets up, throws off his pajama top, and walks into the bathroom. (24

66 *CU of Antoine's face in the bathroom mirror. He wipes some of the moisture off the mirror and the action reminds him of scrubbing the walls of the classroom. We hear Little Quiz's voice say: "I deface the classroom walls . . ." Antoine looks at himself intently, his mouth slightly open. His father enters, smoking a cigarette, and holds up one hand with a sock stretched over it. The sock needs darning and his fingers stick out at the toe.*

DOINEL: Practically no sock left around the holes. *(10*

67 *MCU of Doinel. Mme Doinel enters from the right.*

MME DOINEL: Those are a mess. Buy some new ones; the others are in the laundry.

Doinel throws the sock on a table as Antoine passes between the couple and goes into the hallway. Doinel moves closer to his wife.

DOINEL: Didn't I give you money for sheets for the kid? Hm? Remember?

Mme Doinel lowers her eyes, then looks up.

MME DOINEL: He prefers a sleeping bag . . . (*Her voice grows soft and reassuring as she turns to-*

ward Antoine.) Don't you, little one?

Antoine reappears. (14

68 *CU of Antoine.*

ANTOINE (*eagerly*): Sure, it's warm . . . it's all right. (*He takes some bread and cheese from a shelf.*)

MME DOINEL (*off, sharply*): You still here?

Antoine looks up, rather surprised at the change in her tone, and walks out quickly.
Dissolve. .(7

69 *MS. Antoine runs out of the house and across the street. Music begins, fast and light. René is walking calmly down the street and calls to him.*

RENÉ: Don't run so fast!

ANTOINE: We'll be late. The little door will be closed and we'll have to go to the office and get bawled out.

Antoine walks ahead rapidly, but René maintains his pace.

RENÉ: Take it easy.

Antoine stops and, chewing on his bread, waits for René to catch up. The camera dollies back with them as they walk.

RENÉ: Little Quiz won't let you back. He said so.

ANTOINE: You think he'd do it?

RENÉ: Sure. He can't stand you. (*In English.*) Have you money?

ANTOINE (*in English*): Yes, for the canteen.

RENÉ (*grabbing him by the arm and gesturing toward the other side of the street*): O.K. Trust me. This way out.

They turn right and cross the street. (29

70 *LS of Antoine and René talking excitedly on the*

sidewalk. They turn at the corner and René takes Antoine into an open doorway. They hide their books behind the door and stroll out down toward the great boulevards. (31

71 LS. *The camera tilts down from the Astor Theater marquee ("The White Slave" is playing) as the two come out and move off down the street. With a rapid blurring movement, the camera whips to:*

71a MS *of the two on another street as they go into a second theater. They buy their tickets and the camera tilts up past a corner of the marquee (revealing a white man with a half-nelson grip on an Oriental in a skull-cap) and arrives at the sign "Ciné."* (17

72 LS. *The two cross a street. With mock ceremony, Antoine holds up his hand, stopping traffic. They*

wave derisively at one angry driver and continue across. The music ends. (11

73 *MCU. René and Antoine are playing pinball. Jazz is heard from a jukebox.*

74 *MS from above. The camera looks down into a large wooden cylindrical drum—called "The Rotor" —in an amusement center. Antoine and several other people enter through a door in the side. Antoine presses himself against the wall of the cylinder, his hands in his pockets.* (13

75 *MS from Antoine's point of view, looking up. Several spectators, including René, peer over the upper lip of the cylinder.* (3

76 *MS from above. Antoine smiles as the cylinder begins to rotate clockwise. As it picks up speed, people are flattened against the side walls by centrifugal force. Antoine comes into view, laughing.* (25

77 *MS from below. The faces of the people watching from above, which are of course stationary, appear to be spinning from the point of view of someone in "The Rotor."* (4

78 *MS from above. The cylinder goes faster and faster and the faces and bodies inside it become blurred. Antoine whizzes by, his arms outstretched and flattened against the wall. The centrifugal force induces a state of weightlessness and several people have been lifted off the bottom of the drum and hang against the side, their feet off the floor. The spinning drum roars; some people scream with pleasure or fear.* (7

79 *MS from below. A blur of faces and hats.* (4

80 MCU. *Antoine's face is flattened into a smile. The camera tilts down to reveal his feet, which are way off the bottom of the drum, then tilts back up to his face. In an ecstasy of weightlessness, he begins shifting until he is almost horizontal.* (12

81 MS *from below. Faces whiz by.* (4

82 MCU. *Antoine shifts farther until he is completely upside down, his head pointed toward the earth, his arms flat out against the wall.* (6

83 MS *from below. The heads of the spectators spin by upside down.* (2

84 MCU. *Antoine slowly rights himself. He bends across his legs for a moment, then falls back against the wall, his mouth open, completely overwhelmed by his sensations.* (13

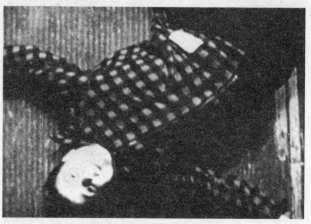

85 MS *from below. Faces whiz by, right side up.* (2

86 MCU. *Antoine struggles to raise his head off the wall but falls back.*
   He tries again and is thrown back again, rapping his head sharply on the wall. He laughs, holding his head.   (8

87 *Same as shot 85.*   (3

88 MS *from above. Antoine shifts till he is horizontal again, but the cylinder has begun to slow down. As the rotation slows, gravity reasserts itself and the riders slide to the bottom of the drum.*   (14

89 MCU. *Antoine slips down the wall with a bounce, exhales in great relief, and runs his hands through his hair.*   (4

90 MS *from above. The cylinder has almost come to a stop. Several people, including Antoine, attempt to reach the pole at the center of the drum but they totter back to the wall, defeated by dizziness and the remaining centrifugal force.*   (6

91 MS *from below. The faces above are recognizable. René spins into view, laughing.*   (5

92 MS *from above. Antoine staggers to the door and pounds on it, going through as soon as the attendant opens up.*   (9

93 MS. *The outside of "The Rotor." Antoine runs down the steps, smiling, and joins René, who has come down another set of steps from the gallery. They go off together.*   (8

94 LS from above. The two walk down a crowded boulevard and turn right.   (17

95 LS from above. A crowded corner of the Place Saint-Augustin. A couple is embracing passionately in the midst of the activity around a métro entrance. Antoine and René pass near them.   (5

96 MCU from behind the woman. She is blonde and is wearing a sealskin coat.   (3

97 CU from the side. The woman is Mme Doinel; the man is a stranger.   (2

98 CU. Antoine and René are crossing the corner. Antoine, looking to his left, sees his mother and starts, surprised. René glances in that direction.   (2

99 CU of the couple, seen from the side. Mme Doinel sees Antoine out of the corner of her eye. (1

100 *MCU. Antoine stares; his expression turns to pain.* (1

101 *CU. Mme Doinel pushes her lover back abruptly and turns away.* (1

102 *MCU. Antoine finally stops staring and ducks his head as he grabs René's arm.* (2

103 *MCU. The couple turns away from the boys.*

MME DOINEL (*distraught*): My God! Antoine! He must have seen me.

The man sneaks a glance at the departing boys. Mme Doinel looks over her shoulder guardedly. (4

104 *MCU of the couple, from the other side. The man watches the two boys while Mme Doinel continues to hide her face.*

THE MAN: Which one is yours?

MME DOINEL: The small, dark one. But he should be in school. *(1*

105 *MS of Antoine and René crossing the street, as seen from behind. Antoine urges René to go faster.* *(2*

106 *MS of Antoine and René crossing the street, as seen from the front.*

RENÉ: You're in for it.

ANTOINE (*shrugging*): You think so? (*Bitterly.*) She won't dare tell my father.

RENÉ: The man?

ANTOINE: Never saw him before.

RENÉ: I guess you're safe then.

They move to the right, out of the frame. The couple is retreating in the opposite direction. *(8*

107 *MS. Antoine and René cross another street and go into the doorway where they have left their notebooks. As the camera pans with them we see Mauri-*

cet hiding behind a tree, spying. Music begins.

René and Antoine come out of the doorway and go around the corner without seeing Mauricet. (23

108 *The two walk into MCU and sit on a small shed behind an iron fence. The music stops.*

ANTOINE: I'm going back in tomorrow (*looking down*), only I need an absence note. What about you?

RENÉ (*reaching inside his coat*): I've got an old one I never used. I'll cut off the date. You can have it to copy.

ANTOINE: Yeah, but what about the handwriting?

RENÉ: Imitate your mother's.

ANTOINE: That's hard. She has a funny pointed handwriting.

RENÉ: Don't worry. It'll be all right.

ANTOINE: I hope so.

They shake hands and Antoine runs off. (30

□

109 *MCU. Antoine is sitting at his dining-room table copying the note. He is nervous and keeps looking up.*

ANTOINE: Will you please . . . excuse my son . . .

René . . . René . . . who has been sick . . . My son René!

He has copied his friend's name by mistake and is disgusted. He gathers up the note and the attempted copies and dumps them in the stove. (33

110 *MS of the hallway. Doinel comes in the door as Antoine appears in the foreground. They greet each other.*

DOINEL: It smells of burning in here again.

ANTOINE: It's from downstairs.

DOINEL (*taking off his coat*): Set only two places.

ANTOINE (*hopefully*): Mama's left?

DOINEL: No, but she called to say she'd be home late. They're taking inventory at the office. (*He turns to Antoine, who smiles and nods.*) The two

of us will cook a dinner for ourselves. (*He takes
off his jacket.*) She said there're eggs somewhere.

ANTOINE: Yes, yes, I know where they are.

They go into the kitchen. (30

111 MCU. *They enter the kitchen. Doinel slips an
apron over his head.*

DOINEL: Did you work hard today? What did you
study?

ANTOINE: "The Hare."

DOINEL: "The Tortoise and the Hare"?

ANTOINE (*taking eggs down from a shelf*): No, just
"The Hare."

DOINEL: Did you answer right?

ANTOINE (*tossing eggs in the air*): I wasn't called
on.

Doinel pours some wine into a bowl.

DOINEL: You have to push, you have to ask questions, my boy, or else you'll never get into the
race. You have to take the initiative in life.

*Doinel takes the eggs from Antoine, who is slightly
annoyed at this lecture. Doinel cracks the eggs in the
bowl while Antoine reaches for more.*

DOINEL: By the way, have you thought about your
mother's birthday? (*Antoine starts at the mention
of his mother.*) It's the seventeenth, you know.
(*Pause.*) I hope you're going to give her something. (*He takes another egg and cracks it. Antoine is silent.*) Antoine, do you hear me? I know
what you're thinking. She's been difficult lately
. . . but . . . she's understandably rather nervous.
Put yourself in her place . . . she has a great deal
to do: housework in the mornings, office in the
afternoons. And we're so crowded here . . . but
we're going to move . . . I'm working on it. (*Antoine looks around Doinel's shoulder at the mixing

bowl.) And you know how offices are. They always take advantage of women. But she loves you, you know.

Antoine laughs derisively. Doinel, who has gotten egg

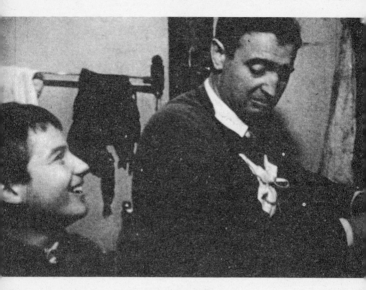

all over his fingers, grimaces at Antoine, throws away the shells, and dries his hands.
Dissolve.[3]   (84

112 MCU. *In the hallway, Antoine lies in his sleeping bag, listening. The door opens and he pretends to be asleep. His father passes by in his pajamas and goes into the bathroom; after a pause he returns and Antoine feigns sleep again.*   (38

113 MCU *of the front door; the bottom of the sleeping bag is in the foreground. We see only Mme Doinel's legs as she enters and gingerly steps over the corner of the bag, closing the door behind her.*

She walks through the narrow hallway toward the bedroom. (14

114 CU. *Antoine feigns sleep. A shaft of light hits his face as his mother goes through the doorway near his head. He listens intently.*

MME DOINEL (*off*): My boss drove me home. I couldn't very well refuse if he wanted to take me home, could I?

DOINEL (*off*): Are you paid overtime?

MME DOINEL (*off*): We'll settle up at the end of the month.

DOINEL (*off*): That kind of work's paid C.O.D. I know Madame needs rest, oh yes! By the way, have you seen my *Guide Michelin*?

MME DOINEL: How should I know? Why don't you ask the kid?

DOINEL: He says he didn't touch it.

MME DOINEL: But he lies with every breath. You know that.

DOINEL: He has someone to take after.

MME DOINEL: If you had raised him better . . .

DOINEL (*furious*): Oh, crap! I gave him a name, I feed him . . .

MME DOINEL (*screaming*): Oh, I've had enough of these reproaches, more than enough! If you don't want to support him, just say so. We could send him to the Jesuits or to the Army orphans—at least I would have some peace!

Fade out. (20

□

115 *Fade in to LS of Antoine running down the Rue Clauzel. Music begins, fast and light.* (2

116 *MS. Antoine crosses the street and waves. The music stops.* (4

117 *MCU. Mauricet is hiding behind a kiosk, watching. He comes out and runs into Antoine's house.* (5

118 *CU. Mme Doinel is sitting at her dressing table fixing her hair. She calls out to Doinel.*

MME DOINEL: All you have to do, then, is eat in a restaurant for the rest of the month. (2

119 *CU of Doinel in his pajamas.*

DOINEL (*vehemently*): To do that I'd have to have a clean shirt to wear! For God's sake, if you don't have time to do the shirt, you could at least do the collar. (6

120 *MCU. Mme Doinel is using her eyelash curler.*

MME DOINEL: If you hadn't bought that fog light . . . (3

121 *CU of Doinel.*

DOINEL (*furious*): I bought it secondhand!

He makes a face at his wife. The doorbell rings, interrupting their quarrel. (2

122 *MCU. Mme Doinel gets up.* (2

123 *CU. Doinel stares apprehensively at the door. Mme Doinel comes into the frame and she appears frightened too.*

MME DOINEL (*finally*): Well? Go open it.
DOINEL: Suppose it's the gas man?
MME DOINEL: No, they notify you first.

Doinel walks to the door. (15

124 *MCU. Doinel opens the door. It is Mauricet.*

MAURICET: Good morning, sir. I'm in Antoine's class.
I came to see if he's better. (4

125 *CU of Doinel, from below; Mauricet's shoulder is in the foreground. Doinel is astonished.*

DOINEL: Better? Why? (2

126 *CU, reverse angle, of Mauricet, from above; Doinel's shoulder is in the foreground.*

MAURICET: He was absent from school yesterday.
DOINEL (*turning to his wife*): You heard? (*He turns back to Mauricet.*) (5

127 *CU. Doinel rubs his face.*

DOINEL: Thank you, young fellow. (2

128 *CU of Mauricet.*

MAURICET: Good-by, sir. (*He pulls up his hood and leaves.*) (2

129 *MCU. Doinel closes the door, walks through the hallway, and stops in CU in front of his wife.*

DOINEL: You don't seem surprised.

MME DOINEL: No . . . I expect anything from him.

She says this as if Antoine's lies erased any suspicion of her own. She turns away from her husband abruptly. He frowns at her back. (17

□

130 *MCU. Antoine and René are walking on the Rue des Martyrs.*

ANTOINE: What am I going to do for an excuse?

RENÉ: It'd better be something big—the bigger the better. Last year, when my mother broke her leg, I told them she was drunk . . . I didn't need a note.

ANTOINE: But I can't say a thing like that.

RENÉ: In any case, we better go back in separately.

ANTOINE: I'll go first. *(17*

131 *LS of Antoine running down the street, followed by René. Music begins. The camera pans to the other side of the street, revealing Mauricet skipping to school. He runs into CU.* *(19*

132 *MS. The students and Little Quiz assemble in front of the classroom building. Antoine sneaks in, his head down, but Little Quiz grabs him. The camera dollies in to CU.*

LITTLE QUIZ *(talking with his pipe in his mouth)*: Ah! Here you are. Extra homework makes you sick, hmm? And your parents fall for it? I would really like to see what kind of note you got out of them. Show me your note.

Antoine has kept his eyes down during this tirade.

ANTOINE *(looking up briefly)*: I haven't got one, sir.

LITTLE QUIZ *(getting angrier)*: You think you can get by with that? That's too easy, my friend.

ANTOINE: Sir . . . sir, it's my mother.

LITTLE QUIZ *(shrugging)*: Your mother, your mother . . . What about her?

Antoine suddenly looks Little Quiz full in the face and takes the plunge.

ANTOINE: She's dead.

Little Quiz is surprised. He takes his pipe out of his mouth and quickly assumes a professional air of commiseration, patting Antoine on the head.

LITTLE QUIZ: Forgive me, my child, I didn't know. Was she sick?

Antoine nods, his eyes lowered.

LITTLE QUIZ: You should have told me. You should always confide in your teachers. (*He pushes Antoine gently.*) Go, go join your friends.

When Antoine goes off, Little Quiz blows the whistle and leads the boys inside. Antoine has fallen in line next to René. His head is bowed and he looks upset.

RENÉ: What was your excuse?

ANTOINE (*tossing his head*): Oh, leave me alone! (66

133 *MCU. Little Quiz is sitting at his desk cleaning his spectacles. He nods at one of the students.* (10

134 *MCU. Duverger begins to recite.*

DUVERGER: "Better than the thorn in the woods . . . the thorn in the woods . . ."

A STUDENT BEHIND HIM (*whispering*): "The thorn where I think . . ." (3

135 *MCU of Little Quiz.*

LITTLE QUIZ: If you washed your ears, Duverger, you
   might hear the prompting. (2

136 *MCU of Duverger.*

THE STUDENT BEHIND HIM: "The thorn in the ass . . ."
Duverger suppresses a smile.

DUVERGER: He's not trying to prompt me, sir, he's
   trying to get me to make mistakes. Now I've lost
   my place. (7

137 *MCU. Little Quiz impatiently bounces his pencil
on his desk and sighs.*

LITTLE QUIZ: ". . . than the flowers in the manger . . ." (3

138 *MCU of Duverger.*

DUVERGER: ". . . than the flowers in the manger . . .
   Better to have freedom . . ." (*He purses his lips.*)
LITTLE QUIZ (*off*): ". . . and constant danger . . ."
DUVERGER: ". . . than slavery . . ." (*He is stumped
again.*) (13

139 *MCU of Little Quiz.*

LITTLE QUIZ (*exasperated*): "With an eternal April . . ." You're an eternal loafer, Duverger. Sit down! Two! (3

140 *MCU. Duverger sits down despondently, folding his arms.*

DUVERGER: I knew it at home. (2

141 *MS. Antoine is sitting with his arms folded, looking very serious.*

LITTLE QUIZ (*off*): Doinel . . . (*Antoine stands up suddenly.*) Oh! Pardon me, my boy. (*Antoine sits.*) Simonot . . .

Simonot, behind Antoine, jerks to his feet. (8

142 *MCU. Little Quiz suddenly looks away from Simonot, in the direction of the door, and gets up. Simonot struggles with "The Hare."* (8

143 *MS of the class, from the front. The camera pans and picks up Little Quiz walking down the*

center aisle. *All the students stand up as he reaches the door. He turns back to them.*

LITTLE QUIZ *(sharply)*: Sit down.

They sit down. He goes out and can be seen talking with several people on the other side of the door. (14

144 *A rapid dolly in to CU of Antoine. He looks fearfully at the door and then turns away, his hand over his mouth.*

The students stare at him maliciously. He looks at the door again. (6

145 *MS. Little Quiz appears in the doorway, crooking his finger at Antoine.* (2

146 *CU. Antoine gets up and walks off.* (6

147 *Dolly in to MCU of the classroom door. Antoine's parents, Little Quiz, and the school Principal are standing on the other side. Antoine approaches the door apprehensively, but before he can go through*

*it, Doinel comes into the classroom and grabs him
furiously by the sweater, near the collar.* (3

148 *MCU of Doinel and Antoine, from the side. Mme
Doinel can be seen staring coldly at Antoine. Doinel
tightens his grip and twice slaps Antoine hard on the
face. Antoine turns and walks slowly back to his
desk. The other students turn to look at him as he
passes by. They all hear the following:*

LITTLE QUIZ (*off*): Sir, I recommend the punishment
be in proportion to . . .

PRINCIPAL: But all proportion is gone . . . This is
out of our hands; only the parents can be severe
enough.

MME DOINEL: He'll answer to his father this evening.

*As Antoine sits down, the camera dollies in to CU
and he raises his eyes, imagining what lies in store
for him.*
Dissolve. (21

149 MS. *Antoine and René are descending some steps beside a stone wall. It is dusk.*

RENÉ: What'll you do?

ANTOINE: No matter what, after this I can't live with my parents. I have to disappear—don't you see?

They arrive at a landing, slowly turn left, and descend the next flight of steps.

RENÉ: Oh, I've seen worse.

ANTOINE: Maybe, but I want to be on my own. (*Shaking his head.*) I'll write them and explain.

RENÉ: Right away?

ANTOINE: Yeah, that'd be best.

RENÉ: Where'll you sleep tonight?

They stop, in CU, at the foot of the steps.

ANTOINE (*looking down*): I don't know. It doesn't matter.

RENÉ: Wait . . . I've an idea. Be at the Place Pigalle fountain in an hour.

Antoine salutes good-by and they separate. The camera stays on Antoine as he walks off in the distance. Dissolve. (46

150 MS *inside a printing plant. A clutter of sacks, machinery, a step ladder, etc. Antoine and René enter. Antoine is carrying a white sweatshirt under his arm. He walks under the ladder as they both walk along the wall of the plant and out onto a balcony. There is a low humming of machines in the background.*

RENÉ: It's an old printing plant—belonged to my uncle. The machines are so heavy the floor fell in.

ANTOINE: Maybe it'll cave in more. (15

151 MCU. *The two come out onto the balcony and*

climb over a railing and onto a ledge.

RENÉ: No . . . it hit bottom . . . anyway, you won't
be cold here. (9

152 *MS. The two walk along the wall next to the
presses. René finds the place he wants and stops. Antoine pulls on the sweatshirt; René throws down
some sacks for bedding.*

RENÉ: Here's a pillow and a mattress. God, it's heavy.
Don't come in until midnight.

ANTOINE (*handing René his briefcase*): Keep my
briefcase until tomorrow.

*They go off. Antoine puts his coat on over the sweat-
shirt.* (34

153 *CU of Doinel and his wife at home. Doinel is
reading a letter aloud—Antoine's letter. His wife
watches her husband intently as he reads.*

DOINEL: "My dear parents, I understand" . . . without the "d" . . . "how serious my lie was . . ."

MME DOINEL: Why did he have me die, rather than you?

DOINEL (*looking up*): A matter of choice, obviously. (*He continues to read.*) "After this, life together is no longer possible for us, so I'll try my luck alone in Paris or somewhere else. I want to prove I can become a man—then I'll return and explain everything. So good-by . . . I kiss you . . . Antoine."

At this last, Mme Doinel moves away.

MME DOINEL: You think his hating me is normal.

Doinel turns to her and again they are both held in CU.

DOINEL: But you are harder and harder on him.

MME DOINEL (*sullenly*): He gets on my nerves.[4] (29

154 *MS. Night. Antoine walks past a boutique, his hands in his pockets, his collar up against the cold. Music begins. He looks up at a mannequin in the window.*
Dissolve. (13

155 *MS. Antoine is walking along the Rue Montmartre. Suddenly a café door opens and a woman (Jeanne Moreau) comes out chasing a small dog. The music stops.*

MOREAU: Can you help me catch him?
ANTOINE (*running along beside her*): Sure.

She runs ahead of him. He passes a man (Jean-Claude Brialy) waiting in the shadows. The man grabs him.

BRIALY: Hey, kid! Is that your sister?

They walk along together.

ANTOINE (*looking back at him*): No, I've never seen

her before. She asked me to chase her dog.

BRIALY: Is it lost or is it hers?

ANTOINE: I don't know.

As they catch up to Mlle Moreau, who has turned back toward them, Brialy pushes Antoine away. He walks in front of Moreau, whistling and searching.

BRIALY: Need any help?

MOREAU: Sure, the more the better.

BRIALY: What's he called?

MOREAU: I don't have any idea.

BRIALY: Run along, kid.

ANTOINE: I saw him first . . . !

BRIALY: Get lost, stupid. (*He runs after Moreau.*) (37

156 *MCU. Antoine passes in front of a store decorated with a "Merry Christmas" sign.*
Dissolve. (5

157 MCU. *Antoine lies sleeping on the sacks in the printing plant, the collar of his sweatshirt pulled over his mouth. He is awakened by the sound of men entering and he immediately gets up, grabs his coat, and runs along the row of machinery. A man can be seen on the balcony above.* (20

158 MS. *It is still night. Antoine walks by a café, as seen from inside. He stops and peers through the window for a minute, then moves on. Music begins.* (15

159 CU. *Antoine stands and looks into the distance, very serious. The camera pans to a man delivering milk: he stacks four cases of milk in a doorway and leaves. Antoine watches, then walks quietly toward the doorway.* (29

160 MCU. *Antoine goes past the doorway, his shadow on the wall behind. The music ends. He*

stops and comes back, turning one case that has been placed on its side so that the bottles are exposed.

He moves away, then darts back quickly, steals one bottle, and runs off. (12

161 LS. *Antoine enters an alley, the bottle under his coat, and walks into MCU. He turns into a doorway, pulls the top off the bottle and takes a long swig, then holds the bottle against his chest, very frightened. He takes another swig, a third, and a fourth, and runs off with the open bottle under his coat. Dissolve.* (53

162 MCU. *Farther down the alley, Antoine looks around furtively, sits on the curb, and begins drinking again.*

He stows the bottle in a sewer drain and walks off. Music begins. (13

163 LS. *He crosses a low wall and goes down some steps into the Place de la Trinité. It is dawn.* (13

164 MS. *He jumps into the lowest basin of a tiered fountain; it is empty.*

He walks to the next level and jumps up, holding onto the lip with his arms. (7

165 MCU. *He holds himself up with one arm while he splashes his face with some grimy water from the basin.* (5

166 LS. *He jumps down and walks out of the bottom basin, then runs across the open area in front of a church and out onto the busy street. The music stops.* (19

167 *MS of the schoolyard. Antoine walks up to René, who gives him his briefcase. They cross the yard into MCU, walking in front of their teacher and a colleague. Little Quiz turns as they go by.*

LITTLE QUIZ: Tell me, Doinel, did you get yours at home last night, eh?

ANTOINE (*turning around to him*): Not at all . . . everything was fine.

Little Quiz waves him away in disgust and turns to his colleague.

LITTLE QUIZ: The parents actually ruin them for us!

The other teacher shrugs. Little Quiz turns and looks at the boys playing in the yard. The camera pans to them. René and Antoine are sitting on the front steps; in front of them a piggy-back fight rages; others are playing in a corner.[5]   (32

168 *MCU. René is standing at the board in English class, facing a teacher who is sitting at his desk.*

TEACHER: Last question—even simpler. (*In English.*) Where is the father?

RENÉ: Ze fazeur . . .

TEACHER: No! Fa-ther.

RENÉ: Fa-zeur.

TEACHER: Fa-ther. The tip of the tongue between the lips. Fa-ther. As if you lisped. (*He pronounces the word again, tongue between lips. René grins.*) Fa-ther.

RENÉ: Fa-zeur.

TEACHER (*striking the desk*): No!

RENÉ: I can't, sir. Not everyone can put his tongue the way you say to do it.

TEACHER: Shut up! (*Pointing.*) S-s-s-sit . . . s-s-s-sit . . . go to your seat!

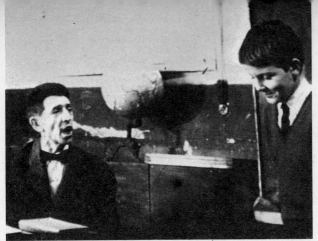

René goes, grinning to himself.

TEACHER: You're insolent!　　　　　　　　　　*(34*

169　*MS. René sits down.*

TEACHER (*off*): Stand up, stand up.
The small tousle-headed boy rises.　　　　　　*(5*

170　*CU of the teacher.*

TEACHER: Answer me. (*In English.*) Where is the
　　girl?　　　　　　　　　　　　　　　　　*(5*

171　*MS of the class.*

BOY (*in English*): The girl is at the beach.　　*(5*

172　*MCU of the teacher.*

TEACHER: No! Beeeach. (*He makes it into a diph-
　　thong.*)　　　　　　　　　　　-　　　　*(2*

173　*MS. The tousle-headed boy turns around as the
Principal appears at the door and knocks.*

BOY: Beach.　　　　　　　　　　　　　　　*(2*

174　*MCU. The teacher gets up.*

TEACHER (*as he walks toward the door*): Beeeach. (4

175 MS. *The teacher goes to the door and talks to the Principal. Antoine is called and he gets up and goes to the door too. Everyone watches.*

TEACHER: Frochot, take charge until I return.

The tousle-headed boy sits, relieved. A studious-looking boy with glasses gets up and the class turns back toward the front of the room.[6]   (25

176 MCU. *The Principal is conversing with Mme Doinel.*

MME DOINEL: We no longer know how to cope with him.

PRINCIPAL (*sympathetically*): Ah, Madame, you deserve better.

Antoine comes in, his head down. Mme Doinel embraces him and turns him around.

MME DOINEL: My poor darling! Nothing happened to you at least! Where'd you spend the night?

ANTOINE (*softly*): In a printing plant.

MME DOINEL: In a printing plant? (*She holds him tighter and turns to the Principal.*) I wouldn't mind his marks if his conduct only improved.

PRINCIPAL: Well, it's all of a piece.

TEACHER (*who has come in behind Antoine*): Maybe it's his glands.

Mme Doinel looks closely at Antoine as if to consider this suggestion, then looks at the teacher, who appeals mutely to the Principal for support.
Dissolve. (28

177 *LS. Antoine and Mme Doinel are crossing a street. She has her arm around his shoulder and bends over solicitously, talking to him as they walk.*
Dissolve. (7

178 *MCU. Mme Doinel is drying Antoine after a hot bath.*

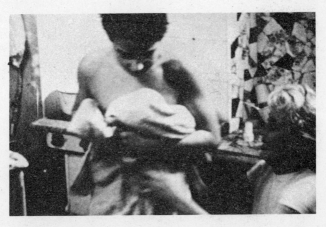

She kisses him and rubs his back, but he averts his eyes.

MME DOINEL: You mustn't catch cold. There! And now to bed.

She pushes him into the alcove and he sits on his sleeping bag.

ANTOINE: But I'm not sleepy, Mom.

She bends over him, taking his face into her hands.

MME DOINEL: No, no. Get in ours, you'll be better off.

Again she pushes him gently, this time along the hallway into the next room. (22

179 MCU. *Antoine enters the bedroom holding the towel around his body. Mme Doinel follows. He walks to the bed, drops the towel, and jumps in. She tucks him in and sits down on the bed.*

MME DOINEL: You know, I was once your age, too. You kids never realize that. (12

180 *CU of Mme Doinel.*

MME DOINEL (*earnestly*): I was stubborn too. I didn't want to confide in my parents . . . (3

181 *CU. Antoine listens intently, his head propped up on an elbow.*

MME DOINEL (*off*): I preferred writing in my diary. (2

182 MCU *of the two, from the side and slightly above.*

MME DOINEL: No one has ever read it—one day I'll show it to you, eh? (4

183 *CU of Mme Doinel. As she speaks she looks away. Music begins softly.*

MME DOINEL: When I was your age I was on a vacation and I went off with a young shepherd . . . puppy love . . . but (*looking at him again*) they caught us quickly. Mother made me promise never

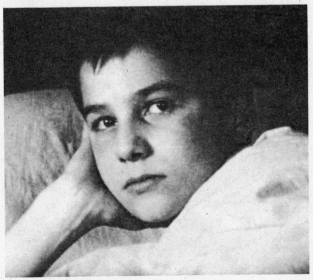

to see him again and she never said anything to my father. I cried a lot, but I obeyed . . . (*14*

184 *CU of Antoine.*

MME DOINEL (*off*): . . . because one must always obey one's mother. (*Antoine looks away.*) Let's share secrets, O.K.? (*6*

185 *CU. Mme Doinel smiles encouragingly.*

MME DOINEL: What did you mean in your letter that you'd "explain everything"? (*5*

186 *CU of Antoine.*

ANTOINE (*shrugging*): About my bad behavior . . . and my bad schoolwork . . . (*5*

187 *CU of Mme Doinel.*

MME DOINEL: Well, tell me then . . . (*2*

188 *CU of Antoine.*

ANTOINE (*shrugging*): I can't pay attention . . . and anyway, I'd rather quit school and work. (*5*

189 *CU of Mme Doinel.*

MME DOINEL (*urgently*): Don't be silly. You have no idea how I regret not continuing my studies . . . And your father, who never got his diploma, huh? It hurt his whole career . . . (*11*

190 *CU. Antoine is listening.*

MME DOINEL (*off, in a tone of perfect reasonableness*): I know they teach a lot of useless things . . . algebra . . . science . . .

Antoine looks away. (*7*

191 *CU of Mme Doinel.*

MME DOINEL: Who needs it? But French, hmm? One always has letters to write . . . (*Smiling again.*) We'll have another secret, just the two of us, O.K.?

(9

192 *CU of Antoine.* (2

193 *CU of Mme Doinel.*

MME DOINEL: If in the next French test you're in . . . the top five, I'll give you 1000 francs. (7

194 *CU. Antoine looks down, then looks up at her again.*

MME DOINEL (*off*): But you mustn't tell your father.

Fade out. (7

195 *Fade in to MS of a gym teacher, in shorts and sneakers, whistle in mouth, leading a double line of boys out of the school at a trot. Music begins.*

He stops at the front gate as the boys jog down the street to the left. The teacher, meanwhile, continues

to jog in place, expelling breath through the whistle which makes a short, rhythmical "peep." When the last of the boys has come out, the teacher races to the front of the line. As he runs, he throws his arms in and out to draw air into his lungs. The whole group recedes in the distance, except for the last four boys, who peel off and duck into a doorway. Then two more. The teacher is completely oblivious to these defections. (28

196 *MS. The tousle-headed boy leaves the group next, snapping his fingers and clapping his hands to his own rhythm. René and Antoine make their escape, dodging traffic as they cross the street. The gym teacher continues to swing his arms open and shut.* (16

197 LS of the group from high overhead. As the teacher leads the group off the sidewalk, out onto the street, four boys dodge behind a parked truck. The remainder reach the other side of the street and three more break off and run in the opposite direction. The camera pans as the group crosses a side street and another three leave.

A bit farther on, one more ducks into a doorway, and the shot fades with the gym teacher trotting at the head of a class of two students. The music ends. Fade out.   (46

□

198 Fade in to MCU of Antoine reclining on a couch at home, smoking and reading a volume of Balzac. An anonymous male voice reads the following.

READER: "Suddenly the dying man rose on his two fists and shot a glance at his frightened children that struck them all like a stroke of lightning. The hair on the nape of his neck shook, his wrinkles trembled; his face glowed; a spirit passed over that face and made it sublime." *(18*

199 CU. The last page of Balzac's "The Search for the Absolute."

READER: "He raised a hand, clenched in rage, and in a loud voice shouted Archimedes' famous words . . ." (3

200 CU. *Antoine, in a kind of trance, flicks his ash as these last words pass through his mind. Music begins.*

READER: " 'Eureka! I have found it.' "

Dissolve. (5

201 *CU of a cigar box full of odds and ends, which is sitting on a shelf. The camera tilts up to Antoine's hand pinning a photograph of Balzac onto the wall. A curtain closes in front of it. The music ends.*

Dissolve. (10

202 MCU. *Little Quiz is writing an assignment on the corner easel; the camera tracks to the front of the easel.*

LITTLE QUIZ: "Describe a serious event in which you were personally involved." (*He walks off.*) (6

203 *The camera dollies to CU of Antoine, his pencil pressed against his lip. We hear him "think" the following.*

SUBTITLE: "Eureka! . . . I have found it."

Music begins. Antoine bends his head to his notebook and begins writing.

SUBTITLE: "The Death of My Grandfather."

Dissolve. (20

204 *CU of Antoine's corner shelf at home. He lifts the curtain, lights a candle, and places it on the shelf; then he drops the curtain. The music ends.*

Dissolve. (20

205 *MS of the Doinels at dinner.*

DOINEL (*in between bites*): The boss sleeps with the
new secretary now. Well-armed, that girl. She uses
her weapons to become executive secretary to the
Director . . . she has all the required aptitudes.
Now we've got to watch out for her—she might
tattle when she's on the boss' pillow . . . I stupidly
used to tell her how to pad expense accounts while
on the road. Christ! She only stayed at three-star
hotels. That reminds me: I still haven't found my
Guide Michelin (*pointing at Mme Doinel*) which
one of you obviously misplaced.

MME DOINEL (*exasperated*): You know, you're beginning to bore us with your *Michelin.*

DOINEL (*leaning across the table*): Well, I don't like
mysteries! (*Looking over his shoulder.*) You left
something on the fire again.

MME DOINEL: I certainly did not.

Antoine, who has been preoccupied with his own thoughts during dinner, suddenly looks up, his eyes widening in horror, and leaps out of his seat.

DOINEL (*looking at Antoine*): What got into him?

(45

206 MS. *The curtain covering the homage to Balzac is in flames. Antoine picks up his pillow and begins battling helplessly at the blaze. His parents rush in, shouting.*

DOINEL: This is too much!

MME DOINEL: Put it out instead of shouting!

Antoine runs off while Doinel flails with the pillow. Mme Doinel clenches her fists and slaps her husband on the back.

MME DOINEL: Get some water!

Antoine rushes in with a panful of water but most of it lands on Doinel.

DOINEL (*to Antoine*): You stupid idiot! That's enough of that!

Antoine, mortified, cowers, expecting a blow. His father grabs him by the neck and bounces him off the wall while Mme Doinel fights the fire with the pillow.

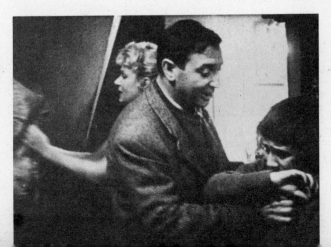

DOINEL: But how, *how,* in heaven's name, did you get the idea of putting a candle there?

ANTOINE: I was honoring Balzac!

DOINEL (*grabbing him again*): Balzac? Balzac? What do you take me for?

ANTOINE: Yes, for the French composition.

Mme Doinel has brought the fire under control. She turns to her husband.

MME DOINEL: Ah, yes. I understand . . . Leave him alone, he promised me something.

DOINEL (*in a kind of frenzy*): What? To collect the fire insurance?

Antoine suppresses a smile. Doinel turns back to him, taking out his pocket lighter.

DOINEL: You'll never make it with a candle, my boy. Do you want my lighter?

He holds the flame from his lighter under Antoine's nose. Antoine, frightened, cowers against the wall.

MME DOINEL (*rubbing her eyes from the smoke*): Oh, don't be ridiculous.

DOINEL (*to Antoine*): While you're living here, you'll do what you're told . . . or it's the military academy for you! (*Antoine looks up in real fright.*) You don't know what that is, my good man, do you? You'll find out, right there on the spot . . . they'll keep you in step.

MME DOINEL (*suddenly all smiles*): You know what we'll do to change the atmosphere? We'll all go to the movies.

DOINEL (*pulling off his jacket, exasperated*): Oh, fine. The perfect method of education.

Doinel leaves. Mme Doinel turns to Antoine.

MME DOINEL: Did you write a good composition?

ANTOINE (*swallowing hard*): Not bad.

She pats him tenderly and turns toward her husband.

MME DOINEL: Listen, Julien, be patient . . .   (63

207 *MCU of Mme Doinel in the bedroom.*

MME DOINEL: . . . he's preparing a nice surprise for us.

Doinel walks up to her, putting his coat back on.

DOINEL: I don't like this!
MME DOINEL: How about the Gaumont-Palace?
DOINEL (*disgruntled*): What's playing?
MME DOINEL: "Paris Belongs to Us."
DOINEL: If this is a plot . . .
MME DOINEL: Would you rather not go . . .
DOINEL: Me? Why? I've worked hard, I deserve it.

Antoine walks up to his mother and she holds him against her shoulder. He is smiling.

DOINEL: But I believe the Gaumont-Palace takes a dim view of arsonists.

Antoine and his mother walk off to get their coats. Doinel looks down and notices that buttons are missing on his coat.
Dissolve.   (26

208 *LS. The three come out of the theater, Antoine in the center. Fast and bouncy music. They are all laughing and chattering excitedly. Antoine looks up happily at his parents. They walk in to CU.*
Dissolve.   (18

209 *MS. Through the windshield, we see them driving home; Antoine is sitting in the back seat. Everyone is laughing.*

DOINEL: And this is the way we punish him!

MME DOINEL: You stuffed him with ice cream, now leave him alone!   (9

210 MS. *The car, a small Renault, goes along a rainy street.*
Dissolve.   (3

211 MS. *The ground-floor hallway of the Doinels' apartment building. A hilarious Doinel performs an elaborate military salute and shouts down the corridor, apparently at a neighbor he doesn't like.*

DOINEL: The Devil's general and his adjutant!

Antoine laughs and Mme Doinel groans in mock disapproval. They go up the stairs, Mme Doinel first, Doinel second, Antoine last. Halfway up the first flight, Doinel lifts one of his wife's legs and shows it to Antoine.

DOINEL: Look what pretty legs your mother has, eh?

She knocks his hat off in protest, he swats her with the hat, and they all run up the stairs laughing. (18

212 MS. *The hallway of the Doinel's apartment. The door opens and everyone comes in, now somewhat subdued. Antoine stands in the kitchen doorway while his parents hang their coats in the hallway.*

DOINEL: Ah, home, sweet home. A little smoky, though.

MME DOINEL (*to Antoine*): Darling, the garbage . . . you're sweet.

Antoine nods and goes into the kitchen.

MME DOINEL (*to her husband*): You see, you see, I've won him over. I hope we won't regret it.

She raises her arms and plays with her hair, watching herself in the mirror. Doinel comes up from behind and squeezes her breasts.

They both laugh, and she shrugs him off gently.
(25

213 MCU. Antoine walks down the stairway carrying the garbage. The music ends.
Fade out.[7]
(2

□

214 *Fade in to CU of Little Quiz holding a paper in front of his face.*

LITTLE QUIZ: If your paper's first, it's because I'm announcing the results in reverse order of merit. Yes, the search for the absolute led you right to zero, my friend. (*He smiles at his pun.*)

To those less familiar with Balzac, I'd describe it as "A Shadowy Affair."

The camera tracks slowly back into the class, away from Little Quiz.

LITTLE QUIZ: It was your friend Doinel's right to choose as his subject his grandfather's death . . . although we know he doesn't hesitate to sacrifice members of his family if necessary.

Antoine comes into view.

ANTOINE: I didn't copy it, sir.　　　　　　　　　(31

215 *MCU of Little Quiz.*

LITTLE QUIZ: Judge for yourself. (*He puts on his glasses and starts reading from Antoine's paper.*) "Suddenly the dying man threw a desperate glance at his terrified children. His hair stood up, his eyebrows raised. His face lit up and became sublime as he cried out Archimedes' famous words, 'Eureka, I have found it.' " (*He reads these last lines faster and faster, in rising anger. At the end he pounds his fist on the desk and leans forward.*) Very well, I've found it too, Doinel!　　　　　(23

216 *MCU. Antoine sits with his arms folded defiantly; he is very glum.*

LITTLE QUIZ (*off*): You're a miserable plagiarist!
DOINEL: That's not true, sir.　　　　　　　　　　(3

217 *MCU of Little Quiz.*

LITTLE QUIZ (*dismissing the affair with a wave of his hand*): Go to the Principal's office immediately. (*Motioning to another boy.*) Colombet, go with him. (*He hands the paper to Colombet and turns back to Antoine.*) (5

218 *MCU of Antoine and René sitting together. Antoine is very dejected; his head is bowed.*

Colombet puts his hand on Antoine's arm and leads him off. (2

219 *MCU of Little Quiz.*

LITTLE QUIZ (*shouting after them*): And tell him I don't want to see you any more this term! (2

220 *MS. In the corridor outside the classroom, a student is rifling the coats that are hanging on hooks. He stuffs things into his pockets, then runs away when he hears steps. Antoine comes out of class and takes his coat. Colombet grabs him by the arm and leads him down a stairway. The camera tilts and through a railing we see Antoine violently tear him-*

self loose. There is a quick scuffle: Colombet is pushed back and Antoine runs away. Colombet hesitates a moment, then runs after him. (14

221 *MCU. Little Quiz sighs.* (4

222 *MCU. René extends his palm toward Antoine's vacant seat.*

RENÉ: He didn't copy it, sir. I'm sitting next to him, I would have *seen* it. (2

223 *MCU. Little Quiz is taken aback by this challenge.*

LITTLE QUIZ: Do you want to be expelled too? (1

224 *MCU of René.*

RENÉ (*casually*): I wouldn't mind. (1

225 *MCU of Little Quiz, now furious. He jumps to his feet.*

LITTLE QUIZ: More insolence! (3

226 *MCU. Little Quiz walks up to René's desk and points toward the door.*

LITTLE QUIZ: Get out!

RENÉ: Sir, I want to be expelled, but I don't want to leave.

LITTLE QUIZ: Pick up and get out!

RENÉ: That's illegal . . .

LITTLE QUIZ (*grabbing him roughly and pushing him to the door*): I'll show you who makes the laws here.

He pushes René all the way to the door, opens it, and throws him out. Then he turns to the class, looks around for any additional defiance, and moves back to René's desk. (18

227 MS. *In the corridor outside, René puts on his coat. Little Quiz comes out of the classroom with René's notebook and throws it up in the air; it flies apart and the pages flutter to the ground. At that moment Colombet returns, without Antoine.*

LITTLE QUIZ: Did you escort him to the Principal?

COLOMBET: No, he ran away.

Little Quiz raises his hands in despair.
Dissolve. (8

228 LS. *Antoine and René are walking along a side street. Music begins.*

ANTOINE: I socked him in the jaw and beat it. What happened to you?

They cross the street.

RENÉ: He expelled me until after Christmas.

They walk in to CU. René puts his briefcase down on a stone wall. They both lean against the wall, very serious.

ANTOINE: You know, after this I can't go home . . . my father told me he'd send me to an academy.

RENÉ: Academy . . . what kind of academy?

ANTOINE: Probably a military academy.

RENÉ (*philosophically*): You'll have a uniform; and there's a future in the Army.

ANTOINE: Oh, sure, but not for me. (*He looks up and muses.*) Ah, if it were only the Navy! I'd love to see the ocean . . . I've never been there.

RENÉ (*eagerly*): I've seen the Channel, the Atlantic . . . (42

229 *MCU of the two, from the opposite side.*

RENÉ: . . . and the Mediterranean, but I don't know the North Sea. Come, you'll live with me . . . We'll manage.

Antoine smiles and they cross the street together and enter an expensive apartment building. The camera tilts to the upper floors. The music ends.[8] (22

230 *MCU. Antoine and René sneak through the*

front alcove of René's apartment. René puts his finger to his lips and they go in quietly. (8

231 *MCU. René closes the door softly while Antoine looks up in wonder. He moves forward, smiling.*

ANTOINE: Holy cow, a horse! (5

232 *MCU of a wooden horse, seen from Antoine's point of view. The camera dollies in to CU of the horse's head.*

RENÉ (*off*): It's my father's . . . a souvenir. (3

233 *LS from above. The room is large, with a high ceiling.*

Antoine pats the horse on its wooden nose and then turns around slowly, amazed at the height of the ceiling.

ANTOINE: It sure is big here.

René is busy removing loose clothing and a wicker

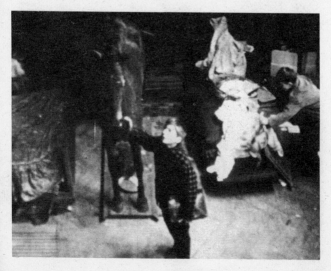

basket full of laundry from a couch. Antoine breaks
his revery and begins to help. They talk in whispers.

RENÉ: Help me get this stuff off. You'll sleep here.

ANTOINE: What about your parents?

RENÉ: They never come here. My mother drinks, and
my father's always at the track.

ANTOINE: First thing is, we've got to figure out a way
to make some money.

RENÉ: Right, the first thing is money. Meanwhile,
I'll take an advance on my inheritance.

They walk cautiously to a door leading to an adjoin-
ing room. René pokes his head through to see if the
coast is clear. They go in. (42

234 MS. *They enter. Antoine examines the ceiling.*
René leads him over to a side table, dumps some
flowers out of a bottle, and shakes out a key. He opens
a small chest sitting on the table and pulls some
notes off a roll.

He puts the rest back. He replaces the key and the flowers in the bottle. Suddenly, hearing a noise, he hides Antoine behind the drapes on one side of the table and hides himself behind the drapes on the other side. A cat that has been perched on the table looks at René. The camera tilts up to a balcony. René's mother closes a door behind her and proceeds down the stairs into the room. She is dressed to go out and hums and smiles to herself as she walks to the side table.

She quickly goes through the same routine with the

flowers, the bottle, and the key, removes the entire purse, and leaves the room. René comes out of hiding, gets Antoine, and leads him out through still a third door. (94

235 MCU. *They go noiselessly out the front door, René making sure of silence by slipping a comb case between the bolt and the door jamb and pulling it toward him from outside as he shuts the door.* (12

236 LS. *The two come bursting out of the house, through the front yard and the gate, and down the street. Music begins.* (7

237 LS. *They come bounding down the steps of the Sacré-Coeur, laughing and chattering. At the bottom of the steps they pass a priest who is completely covered by a flowing black cape, no arms or legs showing.*

RENÉ: How do you do, Madame.

PRIEST (*whipping around*): Little wretch, get out of here.

They continue running and jumping down the steps and out into the street. (32

238 LS. *They run down René's street and into his house. The music ends.* (7

239 MS *from above. René is sitting at the table with his father, who is ceremonious and distant throughout the meal.*

M. BIGEY: Have you seen your mother today?

RENÉ: Yes, when I came home from school.

M. BIGEY: She's arranged for her hours not to co-incide with mine. She's cooking up something nasty. (*Abruptly.*) Where's the fruit?

He gets up and goes into the kitchen. René runs to
the clock on top of a cabinet and moves the minute
hand ahead. Then he runs back to the table, grabs
some cheese and bread, and runs out of the room.[9]
(37

240 MS. René enters his bedroom. He gives the food
to Antoine, who is sitting on the couch reading by the
light of a naked bulb in a small lamp.

RENÉ: Here, take this. (He runs out.)   (8

241 MS. Back in the dining room, René dashes to his
chair and sits down an instant before his father
returns with a bowl of fruit.   (14

242 CU. M. Bigey hands René some fruit.   (3

243 CU. René looks shrewdly at his father.   (2

244 MS of René and his father. M. Bigey looks over
his shoulder at the clock.

M. BIGEY (*starting*): Heavens! Nine-thirty . . . ! I'll be late for the club.

He gets up and quickly puts on his coat and leaves. René pockets several pieces of fruit, resets the clock to the proper time, and runs into Antoine's room. (20

245 *MS. Antoine is sitting amid a pile of clothes, his face reflected in a wall mirror on the other side of the room. René bounds in and hands Antoine his coat.*

RENÉ: Hurry up, we'll miss the newsreel.

They run out.
Dissolve. (11

246 *CU. Antoine and René are sitting in the theater, completely absorbed in the movie. Antoine blows a large bubble with his bubble gum; it pops and he continues chewing.* (15

247 *MS. The exterior of the theater. René and Antoine come out.*

ANTOINE: Great film!
RENÉ: Yeah.

They stop in front of a publicity photo of a busty actress.

RENÉ: Let's take a souvenir. (*He tears down the photo and they run off.*)

Dissolve.[10]   (7

248 MS. *A public lavatory. Music begins. Two stall doors open simultaneously and René and Antoine step out. Antoine swipes a clock from a table, and, as the camera dollies back through the outside door, they leave the lavatory, closing the door behind them. It is the ladies' room.*   (13

249 MS. *Night. The exterior of a busy café. Antoine and René run out and down the street. The music ends.*
Dissolve.   (8

250 LS. *René and Antoine are crossing a snow-covered meadow. They have a little girl with them; she walks contentedly between her two escorts. There is music.*   (9

251 MS. *A puppet show of "Little Red Riding Hood." The heroine protects herself from the wolf with a rolling pin. The wolf peers at her from behind a mushroom. Shouts of warning and fear from the audience.*   (6

252 MS. A rapt audience of young children. One boy
pulls the candy from his mouth so he can call out a
warning against the wolf.   (3

253 MCU. A boy and a girl, probably his sister; other
children in the background. The children are open-
mouthed in suspense.   (3

254 MS. More children in various moods of fear and
hilarity.   (2

255 LS. A large segment of the audience.   (5

256 CU of the puppet show. The wolf snaps his teeth
greedily.   (1

257 MS. The children are looking frightened. One
girl turns away from the stage, seeking reassurance
from her friends.   (5

258 CU of show. Little Red Riding Hood and the
wolf are fighting.   (2

259 MCU. One of the children in the audience
clutches his ears, his mouth open. The girl next to
him stares at him, then turns back toward the stage.
                                                          (5

260 CU. On stage, the battle rages on. The heroine
drives the wolf back with her rolling pin.   (3

261 MCU of two boys, completely absorbed.   (3

262 CU. On stage, the wolf is at bay.   (1

263 MS. Antoine and René are sitting at the back of
the auditorium. They are amused, but are hardly as
absorbed in the performance as the others or as they

themselves would be at the movies. During the following conversation they do not look at each other.

RENÉ: We've got to know what we're after.

ANTOINE: They've got one in my father's office.

RENÉ: Let's get it then.

ANTOINE: We can't sell it; they're numbered.

RENÉ: Don't have to sell it—we'll hock it. My mother hocks everything. *(11*

264 *MS. The audience is shouting and clapping. The camera pans across the crowd, resting for a moment on a nearsighted boy wearing glasses who is struggling to take everything in. The camera moves on.* *(17*

265 *MS of another part of the audience, which is shouting in unison.* *(11*

266 *MCU. On stage, the wolf has put on grandma's bonnet and nightgown. Little Red Riding Hood is being defended by a young man wielding a large stick.* *(1*

267 *CU. A young boy, his gloves still on, sucks his thumb.* *(4*

268 *MS of children laughing.* *(5*

269 *CU. The wolf sways back and forth and then drops dead. The hero gives him an extra knock with the stick. Little Red Riding Hood, a broom over her shoulder, goes off.* *(6*

270 *MS of the same children as in shot 268. One rests his head on his friend's shoulder.*
Fade out. *(8*

271 *Fade in to LS. Daytime. Antoine and René are walking on the Champs Elysée. They go into the arcade which is also the entrance to Doinel's office building.* (11

272 *MS from within. The two walk through the arcade into CU.* (8

273 *MS. Antoine slowly climbs the stairs of the modern office building. He walks from the stairs directly into an office. The lights are on, but the place is deserted. He ducks quickly under a partition, walks through some glass doors, and darts to a typewriter at a desk in front of file cabinets.* (36

274 *CU. The typewriter is heavy, a standard office model. The camera tilts up to Antoine's face.*

He listens a moment to hear if anyone is around, then carries the typewriter away, running through the doors, under the partition, and out of the office. Throughout the shot Antoine is held in tight CU. (15

275 CU of Antoine's feet flying down the stairs. At the landing he turns and hurries on, not hesitating. (7

276 LS. Antoine and René hurry out of the arcade: Antoine is still carrying the typewriter. No one inter-

feres with them and they turn into the street, moving as fast as they can. Music begins. (11

277 MS. A flock of pigeons scatters as they hurriedly cross the street. (6

278 MS. They go down the steps to the métro. (2

279 MS. Inside the modern métro station, René finally takes over the burden of carrying the heavy and

clumsy typewriter. They continue down the stairs to the tracks.
Dissolve. (14

280 MS. *They emerge from the métro in the Place Clichy. A man with a cigarette dangling from his mouth speaks to Antoine, but they shake him off.* (15

281 LS *from across the street. They hustle through the people in the street, cross a side street, and turn at the corner. Antoine bumps into a tall man and turns to apologize. The music ends.* (14

282 MS *from above. They hurry along a quieter back street and René points ahead to their destination. Two men stand conversing in front of a doorway. The boys go on by, but René looks back to see if the men are interested. They stop and come back to the doorway. One of the men walks away. The boys stand talking to a man in a turtleneck and a beret.*

RENÉ: How much?
MAN: Ten per cent . . . and 1000 francs in advance.
RENÉ: Oh no—when you sell it.
MAN: My, my . . . how you trust me.

He takes the typewriter from Antoine and all three walk off together. Antoine and René turn discreetly and walk into the street. (45

283 MS. *The boys walk down the center of the street, as their middleman goes into a pawnshop. They repair to a café on the other side of the street. Once inside, they throw back a curtain that covers the door and watch anxiously.* (16

284 LS. *They watch as the man comes out of the pawnshop, still carrying the typewriter. He crosses the street, looking around warily for René and An-*

*toine; convinced that they have run away, he walks
off. The boys immediately run after him.* (10

285 *MS. Antoine and René go around a corner and
catch up.*

RENÉ (*grabbing the man*): Give us back our type-
  writer! Why did you run away like that?
MAN (*innocently*): I thought you were down here.
  (*He points down the street. The boys frown.*) Any-
  way, they wouldn't take it without a bill of sale.
  (*He edges off, holding the typewriter away from
  Antoine.*)
ANTOINE: Well, give us back our typewriter!
MAN (*obstinately*): O.K. But first 500 francs for my
  trouble.
ANTOINE: We haven't got it.
MAN: You must have something! It's 300 francs, and
  not a penny less.

He edges away but they continue dogging him.

ANTOINE: We haven't a penny . . . give it back.
MAN: Then, my dear friends, that's too bad for you.
  I don't work for nothing, so I'll keep it as a deposit.
RENÉ (*very angry*): The hell! That's *our* typewriter.
ANTOINE (*grabbing the man's collar*): Give us back
  the typewriter, or I'll punch you.

MAN (*brushing him off*): Get your hands off me. It's no more yours than mine. Get it? (*He hears something and looks down the street.*)   (32

286 *LS. A policeman approaches.*

RENÉ (*off*): There's a cop . . . let's ask him.   (4

287 *MCU. The middleman changes his mind and quickly hands the typewriter to Antoine.*

MAN: O.K. Take your machine.

They split up. The middleman walks in one direction, hands in pockets, as if he were minding his business. Antoine and René scuttle across the street, glancing anxiously at the policeman.   (6

288 *MS. Antoine and René trudge along a bridge, disconsolate.*

ANTOINE (*bitterly*): Hell! I'm tired of carrying this thing.

RENÉ: Each takes a turn.

ANTOINE: My father will guess I took it.

RENÉ: It was your idea.

ANTOINE: No, it was yours, you swine! I'm sick of it! I'm going to drop it somewhere.

He starts to put the typewriter on the ground, but René takes it away from him.

RENÉ: Are you out of your head?

ANTOINE (*exasperated*): Oh, all right; I'm going to take it back to the office. (*Holding an imaginary hat.*) But I'll wear a hat so that if the nightwatchman sees me, he'll say it was a man. (23

289 *MCU. Night. René and Antoine walk along the Champs Elysée. Antoine is lugging the typewriter. He turns toward René.*

ANTOINE: Don't be a louse. Take it back for me.

RENÉ (*waving him off*): Not a chance. It wasn't my idea.

ANTOINE: All right, but you're a dirty rat. Here, hold it while I put my hat on . . . and wait for me in front of the store.

René takes the typewriter while Antoine pulls up his collar. They walk across the sidewalk to a dress shop and Antoine jams the hat down on his head. He takes the typewriter and goes off, dressed exactly as always except for the "disguise" of the hat. (21

290 MCU. *Upstairs, Antoine walks into the office, quietly lugging the typewriter to its place.*

Just after he passes in front of an elevator, it stops and the nightwatchman steps out. The camera tracks in to CU of Antoine, who is about to deposit the typewriter on its table. A hand claps down on his shoulder and another pulls up the hat. He is trapped.

WATCHMAN: Oh! Look at this, Doinel's boy—or am I seeing things? Put that down. (*He grabs Antoine by the arm and leads him over to a telephone.*) Papa will be overjoyed, won't he? (*He takes a chair off a desk and sits down, holding onto Antoine.*) And they were giving me a hard time . . . not watching the doors . . . ha! . . . you'll take care of that, because I got you, right? (*He lifts the phone, holding onto Antoine with the other hand.*) And don't play innocent with me . . . I'm on to your kind . . . I don't like little devils like you! M. Doinel? Sorry to disturb you at home . . . Ah, no, but you must come to the office. Let's say it's a

surprise . . . though you won't like it.

He hangs up. Antoine starts to take off his hat, but the watchman jams it back on again, bending Antoine's head down.

WATCHMAN: Don't touch that hat![11] (63

291 *MCU. René waits anxiously in front of the dress shop.* (3

292 *MS. Doinel comes out of the arcade holding Antoine by his scarf, which is pulled tightly around his neck.*

DOINEL: Don't think I'm taking you to a party. The comedy's over—your mother and I are going to have a little peace from now on. (*He jerks Antoine to a halt in front of René.*) Take a good look at your friend and remember what he looks like, be-

cause you two won't be seeing each other for a
while.

*Antoine and René shake hands solemnly. Music be-
gins. Doinel drags Antoine away, pulling the scarf so
tightly that his son's neck is bent to the side.* (19

293 MS. *Doinel pushes Antoine through the people
on a crowded street; several of them turn and stare.*
(8

294 MCU. *The two walk along a quieter side street.
Doinel continues to hold onto Antoine and gives him
an extra push now and then to emphasize his words.*

DOINEL: Maybe this will straighten you out . . . Anyway, this can't go on. If I had done this at your
age, my father would have beat the hell out of me.

*They stop in front of a police precinct station; heavy
wire mesh protects its glass front. The music ends.*

Two policemen are lounging in front of the building.

DOINEL: Can we see the Chief?

One of the men points inside and they go in.
Dissolve. (16

295 *MS. Doinel and Antoine are sitting across a desk*
from the Chief, who is in plainclothes. During this
discussion Antoine keeps his eyes on his father.

DOINEL (*clasping and unclasping his hands as he*
   speaks): We've tried everything, sir . . . gentle-

ness, persuasion, punishment . . . but we never hit
him . . .

CHIEF: Sometimes the old methods work best . . .

DOINEL: But his mother and I—we're not like that
.... we gave him full freedom . . .

CHIEF: Too much, maybe.

DOINEL: No, not too much. But, after all, we both
   work. and you know how it is . . . (22

296 *CU of the Chief.*

CHIEF: Yes, I'm a father, too. Perplexing situations do arise . . . (7

297 *MCU of Antoine and Doinel.*

DOINEL: If only he had wanted to confide in us . . .

Antoine loses interest and his eyes wander to the ceiling. Doinel looks at him and then back at the Chief.

DOINEL: Do you think that when we speak to him he is there? Do you think he's listening now?

He takes the hat, Antoine's "disguise," and claps it on the boy's head. Antoine remains absorbed in the ceiling.

DOINEL: See how I found him with the typewriter. God knows what goes on in his head. (9

298 *CU. The Chief calls an assistant.* (3

299 *MCU. A man comes through a door behind Antoine as Antoine is taking off his hat.* (2

300 *CU. The assistant bends over to receive his orders from the Chief.*

CHIEF (*to Doinel*): You want me to book him? (*To the assistant, quietly.*) Theft and vagrancy.

The assistant nods. (5

301 *MCU of Antoine. The assistant leads him gently out of the room.* (5

302 *CU. The Chief turns back to Doinel.*

CHIEF: Well then, what have you decided? (4

303 *MCU of Doinel and the Chief.*

DOINEL (*scratching his neck*): Whatever happens, right now we don't want to take him back in the house—he'll run away again. Maybe you could place him somewhere. In the country, for example, where they'd make him work . . . (*11*

304 *CU of the Chief.*

DOINEL: . . . because at school he never studies.

CHIEF (*nodding*): All right, we'll try the Observation Center. It's well organized now, with metal shops and woodworking. (*10*

305 *MCU of both men.*

DOINEL: Yes, that's it, that should do him some good.

CHIEF: Provided they have room, of course . . . and for that you'll have to make out an application to the Department of Correction.

DOINEL: Ah!

CHIEF: Yes, so the juvenile authorities can take charge of him. Tomorrow morning, he'll appear before the judge in Children's Court. Only you and your wife need be present.

Doinel takes a deep breath and nods. (20

306 *MCU. In the next room Antoine gives a state-*

*ment to the Chief's assistant, a detective, who slowly
types it out on a form.*

DETECTIVE: "From the fourteenth . . . to the eighteenth of December . . ." (*Someone hands him an empty wire wastepaper basket. He frowns and puts it on the floor on the other side of the desk. He sighs.*) What time did you steal that typewriter?

ANTOINE: Oh, half past twelve, one o'clock . . . but I didn't steal it, sir, I was just borrowing it.

DETECTIVE (*skeptically*): What for?

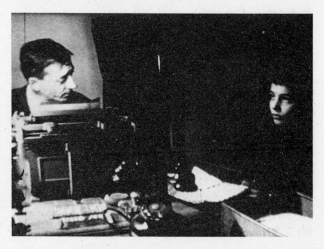

ANTOINE: To write a letter to the Principal so he wouldn't recognize my handwriting. The proof is that I returned it the same night.

DETECTIVE (*nodding*): No one saw you entering the premises?

Antoine shakes his head. The detective reads aloud from Antoine's "statement."

DETECTIVE: "I do declare this day that, having surreptitiously entered . . ."

Antoine lowers his eyes. (35

115

307 MS. *Doinel descends a stairway in the station house, wrapping his scarf around his neck.* (6

308 MCU. *Same as shot 306. The detective finishes.*

DETECTIVE: ". . . I stole a typewriter." Good. (*He pulls the paper out of the typewriter.*) (6

309 MCU *from behind Antoine. The detective slaps the confession down on the table. He hands Antoine a pen.*

DETECTIVE: Sign here.

Without hesitating, Antoine signs it.

DETECTIVE: Charles! Go ahead . . . he's yours now.

A uniformed officer comes in, grabs Antoine firmly by the shoulder of his coat, and guides him through a sliding door into a hall off the detective's office. The officer follows and slides the door shut behind him. (16

310 MS. *The officer conducts Antoine down a stairway. At the landing they walk into CU and the officer delivers his charge over to another officer, an older man.*

FIRST OFFICER: Take care of him. I'm going back. (10

311 MS. *The second officer leads Antoine down a very dark corridor. The camera pulls back and we realize that we are watching them through a small glass window in a security door. The door opens and the second officer and Antoine enter a harshly lit detention room. The officer takes Antoine to a large cage in one corner of the room. A man in a dark overcoat huddles on a bench in the back of the cage.* (19

312 MCU. *Antoine enters the cage warily, hesitating once he is inside. He and the prisoner eye each other cautiously. Finally, the man, who is apparently an Algerian, makes room on the bench. Antoine sits down.*

ALGERIAN: What did you do?

ANTOINE: I ran away from home. And you?
ALGERIAN: Oh, I . . .

The camera backs away, leaving the cage and taking in the rest of the room. The officer who brought Antoine in removes something from a dumbwaiter; another officer reads at his desk.
Dissolve. (35

313 MCU. *The two officers are playing a game involving dice and pieces shaped like horses' heads. A third reads a newspaper. It is the middle of the night. The camera pans across the room to the Algerian, who is sleeping on the bench inside the cage, and on to the corner of the cage where Antoine lies sleeping —on the floor.*

OFFICER (*off*): Ah, the sweethearts . . .

Antoine wakes up. (36

314 MS. *Officers hustle three women, presumably prostitutes, into the cage. Music begins. Two of the women are wearing fur coats; the third wears a dark suit and white scarf.*

FIRST WOMAN: I saw a police station in a movie . . . it was cleaner.
SECOND WOMAN: I've seen one dirtier.
THIRD WOMAN: And I saw one gayer.

The third woman practically sits on Antoine, but one of the policemen pulls him out and pushes him across the room to a much smaller cage, large enough for only one person. Antoine, very sleepy and puzzled, sits down on the seat inside his box. (22

315 CU, *from Antoine's point of view, of the Algerian. The camera slowly pans across the women to the back of one of the officers at his desk. The music ends.* (19

316 CU of Antoine. He pulls the turtleneck collar of his sweater up over his nose and mouth and, crossing his arms, settles down to watch. (16

317 MS. Two officers pull guns out of a cabinet and sling them over their shoulders.

One man goes to the large cage and lets the three women and the Algerian out while the other releases Antoine. (25

318 MS. Outside the station. The prisoners are hustled into a van. It is still night. Antoine gets in last and sits near the back. The door is closed and he peers forlornly out the barred rear window. Music begins. The van drives off. (20

319 LS from Antoine's point of view. The shiny, wet streets and the police station recede into the distance. (5

320 MCU. Antoine sits at the rear window. Other prisoners and police are behind him in the dimly lit

van. Antoine grabs the bars of the window tightly and gazes out at the street. The van moves away from the camera, the camera approaches the van, the van moves farther away, and the camera comes close again. (19

321 *LS, from behind Antoine's head, of the streets.*
(13

322 *MS. The van rushes by.* (8

323 *MCU of Antoine, as in shot 320.* (20

324 *LS from behind Antoine's head. The van passes a large, brilliantly lit nightclub. The marquee says, "The Most Daring Nudes in the World."* (6

325 *MCU of Antoine at the rear window. When he*

exhales, his breath is frosty from the cold. He is crying.
Dissolve. (18

326 MS. *A long corridor leading to a cell. An officer standing in front of the cell turns on the light inside. The music ends.*
Dissolve. (10

327 MS. *Antoine is standing in front of the clerk's desk at the jail. The clerk, his back to the camera, lays an open box on the desk and sits down.*

CLERK: Tie, belt, shoe laces . . . empty your pockets.

Antoine throws the things from his pockets into the box. He puts his feet on the desk, unlaces his shoes, and drops the laces in the box. Then his belt, handkerchief, money, and keys.

CLERK: Sign here.

Antoine bends to sign. A policeman comes up behind him, claps both hands on his shoulders, and pushes him roughly away. Music begins.
Dissolve. (38

328 LS, *from Antoine's point of view, up through an overhead screen into a narrow air well in the center of the building. The walls of the jail end in a skylight. The camera tilts down to a cell window which slams shut.*
Dissolve. (18

329 MS. *Antoine lies awake on a mattress in his cell. He holds the neck of his sweater over his mouth and stares at the ceiling. The camera dollies in to CU.*
    He finally closes his eyes and attempts to sleep. The music ends.
Dissolve. (23

330 MCU. *Antoine is lying asleep. It is morning. A sharp knocking at the cell door awakens him. He closes his eyes again, then realizes he is supposed to get up. He quickly throws off his blanket and walks to the door. The door opens and someone hands him a tin cup. He takes it, surprised at not being let out of the cell. The door closes and he stares through the cell-door window for a minute; he sits down with his cup of coffee, smells it twice, and takes a sip.*

Suddenly he spits it out and dumps the rest on the

floor. He finds a page of newspaper under the bed,
tears off a rectangular piece, and rolls a cigarette
with tobacco left in his pocket. He lights it and leans
back on the mattress, content.   (96

331 CU. An officer's hands guide Antoine's fingers
from an ink pad to the squares on a fingerprint form.
Music begins.
Dissolve.   (6

332 MS. *A photographer gives Antoine a numbered card to hold under his chin for a mug shot.* (7

333 *Extreme close-up. Antoine, his head flattened against the wall, his hair matted and his expression sullen, looks like a little convict.*

Roughly, the photographer turns his face to the side for a profile shot. Antoine shuts his eyes tightly. The music ends. (9

334 *CU. Mme Doinel is sitting in the Judge's chambers. During the interview, she is very nervous and continually fidgets with her scarf and shifts her eyes.*

MME DOINEL: If it came to that we could take him back, but he'd have to promise to change completely. If only you could scare him, Your Honor.

(7

335 *CU of the Judge.*

JUDGE: But that's not my role, Madame. (2

336 *CU of Mme Doinel.*

MME DOINEL: But we can't control him. (2

337 *CU of the Judge.*

JUDGE: Perhaps you exercise control, too . . . inter-

mittently. Tell me, is it true that for an entire
weekend he was left . . . alone at home?   (7

338 *CU of Mme Doinel.*

MME DOINEL (*pausing a moment*): My husband is
busy with an automobile club . . . It's possible we
left the child alone sometimes . . . He hates sports
—he'd rather stay shut up for hours at the movies
and ruin his eyes.   (10

339 *CU of the Judge.*

JUDGE: And what does your husband think of all
this? It's his son, too.   (5

340 *CU of Mme Doinel, her eyes lowered.*

MME DOINEL: No, that's just it, he's not. He married
me when the child was still a baby.
JUDGE (*off*): That's to his credit.

MME DOINEL (*suddenly panicking*): I shouldn't have told you that! *(11*

341 *CU of the Judge.*

JUDGE: Oh, no, quite the contrary. (*Pause.*) Taking everything into account, I think the best thing would be to put the boy . . . *(4*

342 *CU of Mme Doinel.*

JUDGE (*off*): . . . under observation in a center.
MME DOINEL (*brightly*): Oh, could it be near the seashore, Your Honor? *(4*

343 *CU of the Judge.*

JUDGE: Madame, we don't run a vacation resort! I'll do the best I can, depending on what's available . . . He'll remain there two or three months while I study his case, then we'll make a decision. Believe me, this change of environment can only do him good.

They stand and shake hands. Mme Doinel leaves.
Fade out. *(21*

□

344 *Fade in to CU of a large pealing bell.*
SUPERIMPOSED TITLE: OBSERVATION CENTER FOR DE-
   LINQUENT MINORS, C.O.M.   (8

345 *LS. A group of boys in dark uniforms march out
of a large country building that looks like an old
manor house. They line up and sound off their presence.*   (7

346 *MS. A guard comes out of the building and
walks over to three small children who are not in
uniform. (They are apparently children of employees
of the center.)*
   *He rounds them up and locks them into a play area
surrounded on all sides by a high fence. The boys
can be overheard shouting in unison.*   (17

347 LS. *The boys break ranks and run down an incline in front of the building—shouting, somersaulting, and cartwheeling—and out into an open field.*
(10

348 *CU of Antoine and another boy.*

BOY: What're you in for?
ANTOINE: Oh . . . what about you?
BOY: Oh, I slipped.
ANTOINE: I swiped a typewriter.
BOY: A typewriter . . . but that was stupid, my friend.

You were sure to be caught. All typewriters are numbered. (*He turns and points.*) See that big guy over there? He stole automobile tires.

The camera pans to a group of boys who are throwing rocks into the woods; one is taller than the rest.
(19

349 MCU. *Two boys are sitting talking at the base of a statue. The rear end of the stone figure, a lady, protrudes between them. One of the boys strokes the stone buttocks gently.*

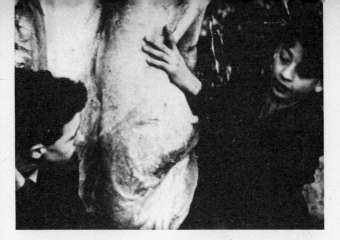

FIRST BOY: Every time I cried at home, my father would take his violin and imitate my crying—just to bug me, you know. But one day I couldn't stand it any longer and boom!—I knocked him out cold.

The camera tilts up to the top of the statue and we see that the lady is embracing an infant or cherub of some sort.

SECOND BOY (*off*): If my old man ever did that to me, I'd kill him. (14

350 MS. *Two policemen pull a tall boy, bruised and disheveled, through the front gate. They march him across the yard.*

SECOND BOY (*off*): Who's that character?

FIRST BOY (*off*): He got caught. He escaped a week ago. You mustn't escape . . . and you mustn't get caught.

A group of boys, including Antoine, fall into line behind the prisoner and the police. An overseer rushes up to the boys.

OVERSEER (*stridently*): What are you doing there? Let's go, double line . . . hurry up, now!

The boys quickly form a double column and the overseer briskly marches them off. The captive boy, marching between the two policemen, recedes in the distance. (43

351 MS. *The two columns of boys, led by the overseer, march past.* (9

352 CU *from the point of view of one of the march-*

*ing boys. The three children have their faces pressed
against the fence.* (6

353 MS *from the point of view of the children. The
boys march past.* (6

354 MS. *The dining hall in the main building. In one
corner members of the staff are being served by a
boy in the standard dark uniform; the rest of the
tables are empty. The marching group approaches,
as seen through a large bay window. The overseer
brings them to a halt and blows his whistle; they
break ranks and run, shouting, into the building.
They stream into the dining room, rush to their
places, and line up behind their chairs. Antoine sneaks
a piece of bread. The overseer comes in last and
closes the door. He pauses at Antoine's table.*

OVERSEER: Let me see the bread.

*One of the boys holds up the loaf, which has had a
piece pulled off one end. Antoine stops chewing but
his cheeks are puffed out; he is caught. The overseer
walks behind him.*

OVERSEER: You bit into it, didn't you? Bring your plate
and the bread over here.

*He walks to the side of the dining room. Antoine
follows, hanging his head. The overseer blows his
whistle and everyone else sits down in unison. He
points to a shelf on the wall, and Antoine puts his
plate on it.* (42

355 MCU. *Antoine turns to the overseer, who holds
out both hands, palms up.*

OVERSEER: Right or left?

*Antoine points glumly to the left hand. The overseer
slowly removes his watch and places it on the shelf,
then very suddenly slaps Antoine hard across the*

face. Antoine recoils from the blow, but composes himself, and reaches up for his plate and bread. He finishes his meal standing up.
Dissolve. (26

356 *MS of the outside window of the cell in which the captured boy has been confined. It is night. Several of his friends have come to visit him. Only his head is visible.*

A BOY: I bet you'd get caught, and I won.

Someone hands him some food and, as he holds it up to his mouth, the camera moves in close.

PRISONER: So what? I had so much fun for five days

that I'm ready to break out again.

A quick tilt down reveals that Antoine is one of the visitors.

OVERSEER (*off*): What are you doing there?

They quickly disperse.
Fade out.   (18

357 *Fade in to MS. A staff member comes out of the main entrance.*

STAFF MEMBER: You . . . to the Psychologist.

He walks to a bench where Antoine and two other boys are sitting and leads one of the boys back into the building. The other boy moves closer to Antoine.

BOY: If she drops her pencil, pick it up . . . but don't look at her legs—or else it goes into your record.

ANTOINE: My record? What record?

BOY: You know, what everyone thinks of you: the

doctor, the judge, even what your neighbors and your parents think of you.

The camera moves close as Antoine puzzles over this news.

BOY: I know my file by heart. I know they've got me down as a psycho-motor unstable type with perverse tendencies. (*He recites this as if he were impressed with the grandeur of the description.*)

ANTOINE: And if I give them a lot of double-talk, just to mix them up?

BOY: Then they'll commit you to Sainte-Anne, and at Sainte-Anne you'll go over the 38th Parallel.

The staff member comes to get Antoine.

ANTOINE (*looking at his friend*): The 38th Parallel? (*The man leads him inside.*) (38

358 *CU. Antoine, hands clasped, is sitting opposite a woman psychologist—whom we never see. During the interview, we occasionally hear boys marching outside.*

PSYCHOLOGIST: Why did you return the typewriter?

ANTOINE: Well . . . because . . . since I couldn't sell it . . . since I couldn't do anything with it . . . I got frightened . . . I don't know . . . I returned it . . . I don't know why . . . just like that.

PSYCHOLOGIST: Tell me, I hear that you stole 10,000 francs from your grandmother.

Antoine looks down at his hands.
Quick dissolve.[12] (15

359 *The same as shot 358.*

ANTOINE: She had invited me—it was her birthday . . . and then, since she's old, she doesn't eat much . . . and she saves all her money . . . she doesn't need it . . . she'll die soon. So, since I knew where she hid it, I swiped some. I knew she wouldn't

notice it . . . and she didn't, because that day she
gave me a beautiful book as a present. Anyway,
my mother used to go through my pockets, and
that night I put my pants on the bed and she
must've swiped the money—because the next day
I couldn't find it. And when she spoke to me, I had
to admit that I had stolen it from my grandmother.
And she took away the beautiful book that my
grandmother had given me. I asked her for it one
day because I wanted to read it, and I found out
she had sold it.

He shrugs, raising his right hand.
Quick dissolve.   (50

360 *Same as 358. Antoine clasping his hands.*

PSYCHOLOGIST (*off*): Your parents say that you lie
all the time.

Quick dissolve.

360a *Same as 358. CU of Antoine.*

ANTOINE (*shaking his head*): I suppose I do, from
time to time. So what? When I tell the truth, they
don't always believe it anyway—so I prefer to lie.

Quick dissolve.   (14

361 *Same as 358. His hands are over his face, his
head is bowed; he lowers his hands and raises his
head. During this shot, his tone of voice is impassive,
completely without bitterness.*

PSYCHOLOGIST (*off*): Why don't you like your
mother?

ANTOINE: Because at first I had a nurse; then when
they had no more money they sent me to my
grandmother . . . but she got too old and couldn't
look after me, so I went back to my parents when
I was eight . . . and I noticed my mother didn't like
me much. (*Wrinkling his nose.*)

She yelled at me for nothing . . . for little things
. . . So . . . also I . . . when . . . when there were
fights at home . . . (*He keeps his eyes lowered and
fidgets with his hands.*) . . . I heard that my mother
had me when she . . . when she . . . well, when
she wasn't married yet . . . and once she had a
fight with my grandmother and I found out she
wanted to have an abortion. (*He finally looks up
at the Psychologist.*) I was only born thanks to my
grandmother.

Quick dissolve. (50

362 *The same shot.*

PSYCHOLOGIST (*off*): What do you think of your
father?
ANTOINE: Oh, he's all right I guess. But he's a bit of
a coward because he knows my mother deceives
him, but so as not to have any fights around the

house . . . nothing . . . he prefers to say nothing and leave it like that. (*He shrugs.*)

Quick dissolve. (18

363 *The same shot. Antoine is looking down.*

PSYCHOLOGIST (*off*): Have you ever been to bed with a girl?

Antoine smiles playfully at this.

ANTOINE (*shrugging*): No, never, but I have friends who have . . . who have gone . . . and they told me if I felt like it I should go to the Rue Saint-Denis. So I went . . . (*he looks up sheepishly*) . . . and I asked some girls, but they bawled me out and I got scared and left. But I kept trying, and once when I was standing there in the street, this guy saw me and he said, "What are you doing here?" . . . Some North African creep . . . So I told him, and he told me . . . he knew a lot of girls because he said to me that he knew one who went . . . a young one, who went with . . . young kids and all that. So he took me to the hotel where she lived . . .

(*he smiles slightly*) . . . only that day she wasn't there. We waited an hour . . . two hours . . . and she didn't come back, so I left.

Dissolve.[13]   (54

364 *MS. A guard opens the front gate of the center and a crowd of visitors streams in. Music begins. The first to enter is René, carrying a package under his arm. Mme Doinel is not far behind: she is smartly dressed and brushes a stray curl under her hat.* (19

365 *MS from the point of view of the visitors. Antoine and several other boys are pressed against the windows of the main building. Antoine's expression is gloomy and apprehensive, but he suddenly brightens and shoves his way past the other boys.* (7

366 *MS from the interior of the building. René is arguing with a guard who sits at a table immediately*

beyond the glass front doors. Antoine runs up to the
doors; René sees him and nods. (5

367 CU. Antoine stands at the glass door. He raps
on the door and shouts: "René!" (1

368 CU. At Antoine's call René turns and again
pleads with the guard, who will not allow him to
enter without a pass. (3

369 CU. Antoine calls to René again, this time de-
spairingly. Behind him another boy watches impas-
sively. (3

370 CU. René pleads with the guard, but to no avail.
(3

371 MS from the interior of the building. Antoine is
in the foreground; René leaves the package with the
guard, turns and shrugs helplessly at Antoine, and
walks off. (7

372 CU of Antoine looking intensely disappointed.
(4

373 MS. *Same as shot 371. Mme Doinel enters the
building and kisses Antoine on the forehead. He
looks through the door after René.*

MME DOINEL: Don't look for your father; I came
alone. (*She points toward a sitting room.*) Not in
there?

*Antoine leads her off in another direction. Other par-
ents rush in and embrace their sons. The music ends.*

(12

374 MS. *René comes out of the front gate, gets on
his bicycle, and begins the long trip back to Paris.
Music.*

(22

375 *CU of Mme Doinel.*

MME DOINEL: Your "personal" letter hurt your father very much. (4

376 *CU of Antoine, his eyes lowered.*

MME DOINEL (*off*): You were very naïve to think he wouldn't show it to me.

He looks up at her slowly. (3

377 *ECU. Mme Doinel, from Antoine's point of view. The camera tilts up to her eyes as she talks, then moves down again.*

MME DOINEL: Despite certain outward appearances, we're a devoted couple . . . and if I've known an unhappy time in my life, it wasn't very nice to remind him of it. It's thanks to him you have a name, no? (9

378 *CU. Antoine swallows hard.* (2

379 *CU. Mme Doinel continues in an accusing voice.*

MME DOINEL: We were ready to take a chance and take you back, but now it's impossible, thanks to the neighbors' gossip . . . you must have told everyone . . . (*She looks to the side to see if anyone is listening.*) (11

380 *CU of Antoine.*

ANTOINE: That's not true, Mother. I didn't say anything. (2

381 *CU of Mme Doinel.*

MME DOINEL: You know I'm used to it. All my life I've been surrounded by imbeciles. Well . . . that's all I have to say to you. And don't try for your father's sympathy by playing the martyr. (8

382 *CU of Antoine.*

MME DOINEL (*off*): He told me to tell you that from now on, he's completely disinterested in your fate.

Antoine lowers his eyes. (5

383 *CU. Mme Doinel pronounces Antoine's sentence in a tone of sweetly enjoyed vengeance. A smile plays on her lips.*

MME DOINEL: All you're good for is the reform school or some place where you'll learn to be an apprentice. You wanted to earn your living . . . Well, we'll see if you like working in iron or wood. (9

384 CU. *Antoine looks up very slowly as if he is trying to imagine his future life.*
Slow dissolve.   (7

385 LS. *The boys are marching to a soccer field. A guard flanks them on each side. Music.* (24

386 *LS from above. The soccer game is in full swing.* (9

387 *MS. Antoine takes control of the ball and kicks it ahead, but a backfield player on the other team intercepts and kicks the ball downfield. Everyone runs after it, including Antoine.* (15

388 *LS from the reverse angle. Both teams chase after the ball, toward the camera. A player kicks the ball out of bounds and a boy on Antoine's team goes after it. Antoine catches up to him and pushes him back, motioning him into position. Antoine retrieves the ball, hustles to the out-of-bounds line and throws it in.*

He takes a quick look around and suddenly darts off the field. As he runs to the fence, the camera pans with him.

He wriggles through a hole in the bottom of the fence, takes one quick look over his shoulder, and is gone. The camera whips back to the field. Whistles and shouts of pursuers. One of the guards races after Antoine while the other holds the rest of the boys on the field. The camera follows the first guard as he squeezes under the fence and then pans to Antoine, who, not too far ahead, runs along the edge of a pond. The guard races after him.   (46

389 MS. The guard runs across a small bridge. The camera tilts down to reveal Antoine hiding at the base of the bridge. When the guard passes overhead, Antoine runs under the bridge and disappears through a hedgerow on the other side. Music begins and continues until the end of the film.   (13

390 *A tracking shot of Antoine running along a road. In one continuous shot, he runs past hedges, roadsigns, orchards, open fields, farm buildings and yards, barbed-wire fences, deserted buildings, a parked truck.*
Dissolve.[14]   *(93*

391 *MS. It is dusk. Antoine rushes down the side of a hill. Beyond him we see an inlet. The camera pans slowly across, past two boats and along the length of narrow jetty. The jetty stretches into the far distance; the open sea is at the end of it. The camera pans past the opening of the inlet to Antoine running on the high ground above.*   *(53*

392 *MS from the shore below. Antoine descends a huge open stairway. He reaches the beach and runs toward the sea.*

The camera tracks back with him. The tide is out and the beach is long and flat. He is alone. He reaches the surf and walks into the water; it circles around his shoes and he looks down, surprised.

He turns and walks in the water parallel to the beach. Taking a look over his shoulder at the sea, he turns back to the shore. The camera approaches him

and the shot freezes into a still—Antoine Doinel, the sea behind him.   (75

Credits

Antione Doinel	Jean-Pierre Léaud
Gilberte Doinel	Claire Maurier
Julien Doinel	Albert Rémy
"Little Quiz"	Guy Decomble
M. Bigey, René's father	Georges Flamant
René	Patrick Auffay

The Children: Daniel Couturier, François Nocher, Richard Kanayan, Rénaud Fontanarosa, Michel Girard, Henri Moati, Bernard Abbou, Michael Lesignor, Jean-François Bergouignan.

With: Luc Andrieux, Robert Beauvis, Bouchon, Christian Brocard, Yvonne Claudie, Marius Laurey, Claude Mansard, Jacques Mondo, Pierre Repp, and Henri Virlogeux.

Special Guest Appearances by Jeanne Moreau and Jean-Claude Brialy

Original story	François Truffaut
Adaptation and dialogue	Marcel Moussy
Director of photography	Henri Decae
Cameraman	Jean Rabier
Assistant	Alain Levent
Music	Jean Constantin
Set decoration	Bernard Evein

Props	Raymond Le Moigne
Soundman	Jean-Claude Marchetti
Assistant Soundman	Jean Labussière
Editor	Marie-Josephe Yoyotte
Assistant Editors	Cécile Decugis
	Michèle de Possel
Script Girl	Jacqueline Parey
Production Supervisors	Jean Lavie
	Robert Lachenay
Production Manager	Georges Charlot
Administrator	Roland Nonin
Secretary	Luce Deuss
Assistant Directors	Philippe de Broca
	Alain Jeannel
	François Cognany
	Robert Bober

The makers of *The 400 Blows* would like to thank everyone who helped in the conception and the production of this film, and particularly: Claude Vermorel and Claire Maffei; Suzanne Lipinska, Alex Joffe, Fernard Deligny, Claude Véga, Jacques Josse, Annette Wademant, and L'Ecole Technique de Photographie et de Cinématographie.

Studio—S.I.M.O.

An S.E.D.I.F. and Les Films du Carrosse
Co-production

This film is dedicated to the memory of
André Bazin

Filmed in Paris, entirely in natural settings, interiors and exteriors.

Shooting time: November 10, 1958 through January 5, 1959.

Running time: 1 hour, 33 minutes.

Premiere: Monte Carlo, May 18, 1959; Colisée, Marivaux, June 3, 1959.

U.S. Distributor: Janus Films.

Prizes: Grand Prize for Direction, Cannes.
   Grand Prize of the Catholic Office, Cannes.
   Meliès Prize (shared with *Hiroshima Mon Amour*).
   Joseph Burstyn Award, Best Foreign Film, judged by the New York Film Critics Circle.
   Medal of Honor of the British Film Institute.

Scenes from the Original Scenario Omitted in the Finished Film

1. This is the way the scenes following shot 42 appeared in the original screenplay by Truffaut and Moussy. They were replaced by shots 43–45.

Rue des Martyrs, 5 p.m. The two boys go up the street.

ANTOINE: I'll never get it finished tonight.

RENÉ: You know I'm king of the subjunctive.

ANTOINE: Yeah, that's something! What a dog, that Little Quiz!

RENÉ: That's his job!

ANTOINE: And the first time it wasn't me!

RENÉ: You got it for everybody.

ANTOINE: It isn't fair.

They arrive in front of the Loinod's* apartment house and go in.

ANTOINE (*fearfully*): Quiet on the stairs or the concierge will yell.

Loinod apartment. Evening. Antoine and René enter.

RENÉ: Say, you haven't got that much room in your house.

ANTOINE: We're still supposed to move. Some chance.

---

* In the film the name was changed to Doinel.—*Eds.*

It's the same as my adenoids operation, some time but not now.

RENÉ: I've still got my adenoids too.

ANTOINE: Open your mouth, let's see.

RENÉ: You can't see them, dope! You've got them mixed up with tonsils!

ANTOINE (*changing the subject because he is wrong*): Come on, we'll get the table set.

They go into the dining room. There is money and a note on the table.

RENÉ: Look at that, money!

ANTOINE: Don't get excited, it's to buy things. (*We see the note "For Antoine" and the list.*) Sorry, it's going to be a while.

On the Rue Clauzel. Antoine pulls out his handkerchief and loses the note, which was in his pocket.

The Rue Clauzel. In front of a grocery. Several women are in front of the boys, whose faces show their discomfort at hearing the following dialogue:

FIRST WOMAN: . . . Yes, they had to use instruments. It was a breech birth. You see, it sort of runs in the family; it seems it was the same way for his mother.

SECOND WOMAN: Oh, that doesn't mean a thing. Look at me: for my first, it was all over in ten minutes. But for the little one, if they hadn't made a Caesarean, I wouldn't be here to talk to you now.

FIRST WOMAN: And my sister, one every year; imagine that. "The next one, you're done for," the doctor said. In the end they took everything out of her, and a good thing too.

ANTOINE: Nuts, I've lost the note.

RENÉ: You know about getting bawled out?

ANTOINE: What am I going to buy?

RENÉ: You know about salad, you know about sardines?

160

ANTOINE: I know my mother.

The Loinod apartment. In the kitchen, René helps empty the basket; in addition to bread and salad, there is an impressive number of cans.

RENÉ (*maliciously*): Well, that'll hold her for a while.

ANTOINE (*petrified*): I didn't think we bought that much.

RENÉ: Don't worry. Women always like to have things on hand.

ANTOINE: I'd better put them away, or I'll get it.

RENÉ: She's a real terror, your mother!

ANTOINE (*as René passes the cans to him*): Beat it. She'll be coming in a half-hour, and I don't want her to find you here.

The Loinod dining room. Antoine is doing his conjugations as fast as he can write.

ANTOINE (*grumbling*): And meanwhile Little Quiz is taking it easy.

RENÉ: Some chance! He's correcting papers.

ANTOINE: Before I go into the service, I'm going to break his neck.

RENÉ: They'll put you in a disciplinary unit.

ANTOINE: I'll join the parachutists.

RENÉ (*looking in the mirror, pleased with himself*): You're too little.

ANTOINE: "Que je degrada . . ." Is that the imperfect?

RENÉ: ". . . dasse."

ANTOINE: "Que je dégradasse les murs de la classe . . . Oh, dégueulasse." Then he'll say I'm writing poetry again, the brute.

René, still looking at the mirror, feels the back of his head.

RENÉ: You know, I think my head is bigger than yours.

ANTOINE (*unperturbed*): Not as much as all that.

RENÉ: That's important because of the weight of the brain. I read that in a book. All great men's brains are heavier than other people's.

ANTOINE (*interested*): How do they know that when they're dead?

RENÉ: They calculate the volume from their portraits and the capacity of the skull. Napoleon and Galileo were the biggest.

ANTOINE: I've got more than you have.

RENÉ: Women always have smaller ones . . .

The noise of a lock or a door.

ANTOINE: Here's Mama.You beat it right away, O.K.?

He rushes to put his paper away in his briefcase as quickly as he can. Enter Mme Loinod, visibly nervous. She looks scornfully at René.

ANTOINE: Evening, Mama.

Antoine takes his chum to the door, unobtrusively.

RENÉ (*in a low voice*): S'long.

ANTOINE (*ditto*): S'long.

2. These two scenes followed shot 48 in the original screenplay.

The Rue Clauzel, Place Breda. 7 p.m. Antoine comes running up to the bakery. It is closed.

The Loinod kitchen. Mme Loinod is cleaning a fish over the sink. Antoine enters, embarrassed.

MME LOINOD: How about that flour?

ANTOINE: The bakery's closed.

MME LOINOD: Go borrow some from the concierge. (*Antoine looks crushed.*) What's the matter?

ANTOINE: It smells bad at the concierge's.

MME LOINOD: Do you think I have fun cleaning fish? You have to learn to force yourself to do things, my boy. Especially when you're in the wrong.

Antoine goes out without saying anything. Mme Loinod takes the insides out of the fish, looking disgusted.

3. This scene followed shot 111 in the original screenplay.

Loinod apartment after dinner. Loinod is all over the table with his maps and the usual material. He laughs to himself.

LOINOD: Am I going to get them! At the Saclay Cross there isn't one of them that's going to make it. (*He looks for something on the table, then gets up to search the shelves.*) Antoine!

ANTOINE (*looking up from a picture magazine*): Yes Papa?

LOINOD: What did you do with my *Guide Michelin*?

ANTOINE: I didn't touch it.

LOINOD: Antoine, you know I can't stand lying.

ANTOINE: But Papa, it's the truth.

LOINOD: I'm sure I put it back yesterday.

ANTOINE (*on the verge of tears*): I swear it's not me.

LOINOD: Well, then I don't get it. Things just disappear in this house.

ANTOINE: I didn't.

LOINOD: All right, all right, I'll ask your mother. (*He looks at his watch and cannot hold back a little gesture of irritation and discontent. Then, mollified:*) It's bedtime.

4. This section was a continuation of shot 153.*

GILBERTE: As he grows up, he's turning into a real nuisance; he admits that himself.

---

* M. and Mme Doinel's first names are Julien and Gilberte.—*Eds.*

JULIEN: He has to express himself—he needs that.

GILBERTE: The apartment won't take it, that's the trouble. It isn't getting any bigger.

JULIEN: You know very well that I'm doing something about that, and more than you think.

GILBERTE: Yes, you're on the trail of something. I know that song.

JULIEN: Exactly.

GILBERTE: It runs out in the sand, that trail of yours.

JULIEN: Anyway, for all the time you spend in the house . . . It isn't a wife I have, but a real traveling pigeon.

GILBERTE: If your position let me, I'd stay home. But instead of improving it, you'd rather waste your time on that washout of a club.

JULIEN: Rallyes, they make friends. You'll see when I'm elected vice-president of the first section.

GILBERTE: You'll never be vice-president. They need you as secretary, to do all the work. But you can keep on waiting for the honors!

JULIEN: You mean to say I'm no good. But then why did you marry me? To bring up your kid, eh? Now the kid is beginning to understand.

GILBERTE: Did he say something to you?

JULIEN: No, but he underlined *everything*. "I'll explain *everything*."

GILBERTE: It's just something a child says when he wants to create a mystery.

JULIEN: If he underlined it, it was because he had something in mind.

GILBERTE: Ah, you know all about him, don't you? He likes to underline everything. In his notebooks and in his letters. (*She gets up and goes to a drawer. She shows her husband a letter.*) Take a look at this. When he was at your sister's on vacation: "You can buy me half a pound (underlined twice) of dried bananas" and later on "Send me 200 francs more and that will be all" (underlined).

What does that prove?

JULIEN: That he was starving to death at my sister's? Is that what you mean?

GILBERTE: You simply don't want to understand!

JULIEN: If you know him so well, you must know where he is tonight.

GILBERTE: Maybe he's at his grandmother's. "In Paris or somewhere else." That might mean at her house. You ought to go see.

JULIEN: Certainly not. If he's there, he's all right. And if he's sleeping out in the open, it'll teach him to take care of himself.

GILBERTE: In other words, things are settled as far as you are concerned. You don't care.

JULIEN: I may not be such a good detective as you are, but I know how to read a letter, including the postscript.

GILBERTE: I didn't see it. Where was that?

JULIEN (*showing the other side of the letter*): On the back. "P.S. But I solemnly promise to complete my schooling." You don't have to worry about that, he'll complete it in the same place, that wise guy.

5. This scene followed shot 167.

The Loinod apartment. Daytime. The father is sleeping; the mother shakes him.

GILBERTE: Julien!

JULIEN: What is it?

GILBERTE: The kid!

JULIEN (*grumbling*): Is he back?

GILBERTE: I wish he was.

Julien turns over, trying to go back to sleep.

GILBERTE (*pulling the blanket off him*): Remember, you were going to the school, "just for luck," to look for him.

JULIEN (*peevishly*): What an idea, getting people up like that! (*Sitting on the bed.*) Christ, if I find him, he'll get it.

6. This was the way shots 175 through 177 appeared in the original screenplay.

A classroom. Daytime. Everything is going along normally. Suddenly, the Principal's face appears at the little windows in the door. Everybody looks in that direction; the Principal beckons to the teacher to come out into the hall. We see that the Principal is not alone, but from where we are we cannot see who is with him. The door is opened slightly. Antoine is called out. As he goes toward the door, he sees his father (the camera follows him, obliquely). All the boys watch Antoine; through the chink in the door, a pair of resounding slaps are heard. Then:

JULIEN: With your permission, M. Principal, I'll take him home, in view of his condition. His mother made me promise that.

PRINCIPAL: Ah, poor Mme Loinod, she must be eating her heart out!

The camera follows Julien and Antoine in the street.

The Loinod apartment. Noon. Julien enters pushing Antoine roughly before him.

JULIEN: Here's your vagrant. Now we'll find out what's what . . .

Gilberte, dressing gown flying, dashes to her son and embraces him passionately.

GILBERTE: Antoine dear, my child, my treasure. What a state you're in! At least nothing happened to you?

JULIEN (*aside*): Huh!

166

GILBERTE: Where did you sleep, dear?

ANTOINE (*almost inaudibly*): In a printing plant.

GILBERTE: Good Lord, I hope he didn't catch cold! (*She goes toward the kitchen.*) I'm keeping some coffee warm. Have a cup and then I'll put you to bed.

JULIEN: That beats everything. (*Shouting at the kitchen door.*) Is that what you call the principles of education?

GILBERTE (*returning*): His health comes first. (*To Antoine.*) Drink it while it's hot. We'll have time to explain things later . . . the two of us.

JULIEN: That's just fine. I get it. (*He exits, slamming the door.*)

7. This scene followed shot 213. Compare the last five lines with shots 195–197.

The classroom. A silent picture of Little Quiz in a rage.

COMMENTATOR:* Things got worse at school. The teachers had told us so often that we were the worst class in the history of the supplementary course that they had convinced us, and we meant to justify our reputation . . . Antoine was a marked man, of course, and no matter how he tried, he could not always avoid the thunderbolts that fell from the heights of the desk . . .

Little Quiz dashes forward and overturns the easel.

COMMENTATOR: It was at this time that Bertrand Mauricet officially received the title of "Stoolpigeon No. 1," and at the same time his vileness was cruelly punished.

---

* There was occasional commentary to be spoken by René in the original; all of this was dropped in the final film.—*Eds.*

Methodical sadistic destruction, by the entire class, of the underwater goggles.

COMMENTATOR: The singing class was an outlet for our most martial instincts.

A mimed song, with increasing drive, accompanied by a gradual encirclement of the singing teacher.

COMMENTATOR: "And the Gauls, the Gauls
 In resounding voices
 Sing a hymn to liberty!"

COMMENTATOR: And Saturday gym was undermined from the outset:
 "The day they started out as thirty, and stole away
 And only three reached the stadium."

Accelerated images of this disappearing act.

8. In the original screenplay, these scenes followed shot 229; shots 230 through 233 were not in the original script.

Main staircase of the Bigey apartment house. Daytime. René and Antoine arrive at the main entrance.

RENÉ: Wait here for me. You'll get the idea in five minutes. If anyone passes by, make as if you were selling tuberculosis seals.

ANTOINE: I don't have any more.

RENÉ (*taking a worn book of stamps out of his pocket*): Here!

ANTOINE: But they're out of date! There's about two hundred francs, or even more.

René runs down the stairs.

The Bigey apartment.

RENÉ: Evening, Toute Belle.

TOUTE BELLE: Good evening, dear. Have you seen Pompon?

RENÉ: No, not since this morning.

TOUTE BELLE: He lives here less and less. I think he must have found a tawny cat. (*Dreamily.*) Tawny cats always make them lose their heads . . . Are you going out?

RENÉ: Yes.

TOUTE BELLE: If you think of it, go to the Italian sausage shop and bring us some salami. (*She takes money out of her bag and gives it to her son.*) Here.

RENÉ: Thanks. (*He goes off toward the door.*)

TOUTE BELLE (*in the distance*): And if you see Pompon, bring him back too.

RENÉ: Right. Good-by! (*He slams the door, but from the inside, after letting Antoine in.*)

9. In the original script, this was an addition to shot 239.

M. BIGEY: Would you want to do something about her for me? (*Pause.*) Don't worry: I'll appreciate it.

RENÉ: Yes, of course.

M. BIGEY: You would have to give her this paper to sign . . . Wait a second . . . (*He takes it out.*) Here it is . . . Naturally, it would be better if you managed to pick a time when her understanding is a little—blunted . . . You see what I mean?

RENÉ: Yes. But you know, it only has to come from you and she's suspicious.

M. BIGEY: She's very fond of you. Do a little wheedling and coaxing . . . O.K.?

RENÉ: I'll try.

M. BIGEY: It's in your interest as well as mine. Without this signature, she can take it into her head to sell the apartment and put us out into the street, overnight. So, be nice, eh? (*He gives René a piece of paper and looks at the clock.*) . . .

10. In the original script, these scenes followed shot 247. Shots 248 through 275 were not in the original.

René's room. Night.

COMMENTARY: We spent the night playing backgammon and smoking my father's cigars. We slept in the daytime on the banks of the Seine, liberated at last from the tyranny of the tenses. I had put two armchairs end to end as a bed for Antoine, and lent him his first long trousers. One night we laughed so loud and long it almost gave us away.

The sound of a door. They disperse the smoke with a blanket, put the backgammon set away, and push the chairs apart. Antoine creeps under the bed. The steps come closer. M. Bigey opens the door.

M. BIGEY: What's going on here? It smells like a smoking lounge—you'd think you were in a den of thieves. (*Picking up a butt.*) My cigars! I thought, after all, your mother couldn't . . . You're going to be as sick as a dog.

RENÉ: Oh no!

M. BIGEY: Oh, you've made it a habit then.

RENÉ: No, it's only the second one.

M. BIGEY: Why aren't you in bed at this time of night?

RENÉ: I was studying my history lesson.

M. BIGEY: And that made you laugh? That's the only subject that might give you a feeling of respect for the French tradition. After all, who produced France if it wasn't the kings?

RENÉ: Well, you know, we produce Pharaohs.

M. BIGEY: Very good. I'll hold back the price of three cigars from your pocket money.

RENÉ: Yes, Papa.

M. Bigey catches a glimpse of Antoine's feet sticking out from under the couch.

The Loinod apartment. Daytime. Julien is shaving, still looking sleepy.

GILBERTE: Julien! The garbage!

JULIEN: What about the garbage?

GILBERTE: It hasn't been taken out for three days.

JULIEN: I can only do one thing at a time.

GILBERTE: Me too. Since the boy left . . . (*She breaks off, embarrassed.*)

JULIEN (*facetiously*): The garbage can is running over, eh?

GILBERTE: Naturally, with worrying, everything is difficult. It really is time for you to try to find him.

JULIEN: It was I who went to the school, wasn't it?

GILBERTE: You have to go to that René Bigey's house. I've only seen him once, but that was enough for me to know what he was like: a first-class crook.

JULIEN: His parents have taken him out of school.

GILBERTE: Now you're telling me! You should have gone to see them right away.

JULIEN: You know I had the committee. I had to give them the annual report.

GILBERTE: Listening to you, you'd think it was the Bank of France.

JULIEN: You can't see farther than your nose.

GILBERTE: Look, tomorrow's Sunday. Thank heaven, there's no rallye. Take advantage of that to go see those Bigeys.

The Bigey apartment balcony. Daytime.

COMMENTARY: Sunday, around noontime, we were very busy with experiments in ballistics.

René is bombarding the passers-by with a bean-shooter.

RENÉ: Give me the *Guide Michelin!*

ANTOINE (*tearing out pages*): The pages are thinner than in the medical dictionary.

Through the window we see a family in Sunday clothes. A little girl has picked up a horribly dirty poodle.

MOTHER: Come on, Madeleine, you're not going to take *that* into the restaurant. What would people say?

MADELEINE: I do want to take him. He's hungry.

MOTHER: You can bring something back for him.

MADELEINE: It's not the same thing. He wants to eat with us.

MOTHER: Mado, be reasonable, just once, and leave that dog here.

MADELEINE: No! No! No!

FATHER (*to the mother*): I don't know why you argue with her. (*To Madeleine.*) Do you want a spanking?

Madeleine goes into a tantrum and says tearfully:

MADELEINE: Don' wanna go without Totor, don' wanna go without Totor, and I'm not hungry, so there.

MOTHER: Mado, you'll be sorry.

FATHER: Oh, leave her. Since she isn't hungry, we'll save some money.

The parents leave. The mother returns, having intentionally forgotten her gloves.

MADELEINE (*talking to the dog*): Nice Totor . . . We'll stay here, just the two of us, and then I'm going to wash you.

MOTHER: Then you're not coming with us?

Madeleine doesn't answer. Her mother leaves again. Madeleine hides and watches her parents crossing the street. She goes out on the balcony and advertises her presence to the neighborhood.

MADELEINE (*screaming*): I'm hungry! I'm hungry!

Windows open.

WOMAN NEIGHBOR: What is it, little girl?

172

MADELEINE: Father and Mother went out to the restaurant and didn't want to take me. I'm hungry!

Indignant murmurs. (1) "Isn't it a shame?" (3) "Some people just shouldn't have children." (5) "Every day in the paper you read about victimized children."

René and Antoine join in the chorus, their voices entering in the following order:

ANTOINE (2): Child-killers!

RENÉ (4): The dogs!

ANTOINE (*imitating the neighbor*): Isn't it a shame?

RENÉ: We have to do something for her. (*To Madeleine.*) Wait a second!

They go back in, toss her a cord, and set up an apparatus to pass her provisions.

Madeleine's apartment.
Left alone, Madeleine opens another window and watches her parents cross the street, still hiding from them. She is thoughtful for a moment, then lifts her head, puts Totor in front of the window, and goes back onto the balcony. In the opposite apartment a little boy, also alone, goes through some grimaces to distract Madeleine, who enjoys them enormously. The little boy is flattered and keeps on. From time to time he disappears and comes back with accessories: hammer, screwdriver, electrician's tape, wires. He imitates the scalp dance, hara-kiri, various animals. While he is wrapped in a bedsheet, majestic as a Roman emperor, his mother enters, cuffs him, and closes the window, after a threatening gesture to Madeleine, who sticks her tongue out, as if to have the last word. The camera comes back to René. We hear the parents returning and asking Madeleine whether she is hungry.

MADELEINE: No, no, and anyway, I ate some cookies!

Her parents look toward René's window, which he closes hurriedly. Antoine laughs.

COMMENTARY: This generous action having cost us our lunch, we had only one recourse: to make some caramel.

An image of a pot with a fire under it.

COMMENTARY: To cool it, there was the marble of the fireplace. There it "set"—so well that it took a horse-racing trophy of my father's to try to break it.

ANTOINE: Come on! A real wallop!

RENÉ: Oh, nuts! (*The statue of the horse has broken.*)

ANTOINE: What are we going to do?

RENÉ (*looking at the caramel*): There are some bits anyway.

They suck on the bits of caramel.

ANTOINE: That makes you thirsty. Is the apéritif all gone?

René shows him the empty bottle.

RENÉ: Nothing! Let's go look in the kitchen. (*They go into the kitchen. René points to the milk on table.*) It's for the cat. You can drink it.

Antoine drinks right from the pot, while René uncorks a bottle. The cat comes up begging, tail in air.

RENÉ: Hey, Pompon, want a drink? (*The cat rubs against him.*) Wait, pretty cat, wait, my beauty . . . Hold him a while. Going to make him a little cocktail. (*He pours the apéritif into what is left of the milk in the pot.*) There you are. Drink hearty, Pompon, drink, my cat . . .

Outside Bigey apartment house. Daytime. Toute Belle is saying good-by to two of her friends, as prehistoric as she is herself.

TOUTE BELLE: Good-by, dears.

FIRST FRIEND: Thursday as usual, eh?

SECOND FRIEND: We could see *Mayerling* again.

TOUTE BELLE: It's not Charles Boyer anymore, you know.

SECOND FRIEND: But the story is so lovely!

TOUTE BELLE: Good-by, girls! (*She makes a romantic gesture to them from the top of the steps before going in.*)

The Bigey apartment. The cat is drunk and slips on the tiled floor. The boys laugh their heads off, and Toute Belle surprises them.

TOUTE BELLE: What have you done to Pompon? (*To the cat.*) Come to see Toute Belle! (*The cat runs away, and she almost falls trying to catch him.*) You've got him in a fine state. (*She is a bit drunk herself. She points at Antoine.*) And that young man? Why is he here?

RENÉ: He came to spend the afternoon with me.

TOUTE BELLE: Is he some kind of actor?

RENÉ (*not understanding*): Uhh . . . he's a pal!

TOUTE BELLE: There's nobody like your Bohemians to torture animals.

Antoine is terrified. René signals to him not to take it too hard.

TOUTE BELLE (*to Antoine*): You must never hurt animals, my boy . . . (*Seeing the mantelpiece and the horse.*) Not even in bronze! Claudion's horse! Good for him! But you're going to catch it, you know, René.

RENÉ: Yes, it's a nuisance. We could hide it.

TOUTE BELLE: He'd notice it. It's a statue of a horse he was very fond of. Star of Aran. An English name. But that horse was so expensive he only owned half of him. (*Holding it up.*) Oh! It's just too funny! (*She laughs uproariously.*) Are you going to get it, my poor René!

ANTOINE: It's my fault too.

TOUTE BELLE: Ah, are you both guilty? Well, I can repair it. I have a special cement.

RENÉ: Oh, Toute Belle, do that for us, do.

TOUTE BELLE: But on one condition. (*To René.*) If you go to the grocer's—not the Italian, you know, the other one on the corner—and bring me a bottle of "mad wine." I'm dying of thirst.

RENÉ: O.K. (*He takes Antoine with him.*)

TOUTE BELLE (*from a distance*): At your expense, of course. (*Lower voice.*) And don't say it's for me.

The camera follows the boys down the hall.

ANTOINE: It must have been a fine horse.

RENÉ: And how! That's why we're broke.

The landing outside the Bigeys' apartment. Daytime. Julien Loinod is at the door.

JULIEN: . . . I beg your pardon, Ma'am . . . on Sunday . . . but I thought it was just the day I would have a chance of finding you in and perhaps . . . through your son . . .

TOUTE BELLE: He isn't here. He's at the races with his father.

JULIEN: Since he left school on the same day as my son . . .

TOUTE BELLE: Well, well . . . He had a right to, didn't he?

The two boys come back with the wine, see Julien's back and stop. Toute Belle has seen them.

JULIEN: Yes, to be sure, but if you had an idea . . .

TOUTE BELLE: I have one. Come in. (*She does not close the door after her, but makes a sign of complicity to the boys, who go up one flight.*) You see: to understand is to love.

JULIEN: Pardon me?

TOUTE BELLE: Do you love your son enough?

JULIEN: Why, Madame . . .

TOUTE BELLE: Why not face it? Examine your conscience. Every time his little soul, thirsty for tenderness, turned toward you like a corolla around the sun, did you answer his appeal?

JULIEN: His little soul! If you knew the kid!

TOUTE BELLE (*laughing*): The Loinod boy?

JULIEN (*furious*): Oh yes, it's a good joke, eh?

TOUTE BELLE: I know him. The last time I saw him . . .

JULIEN: Do you remember when?

TOUTE BELLE: It must have been last week. It was easy to see that that boy has not blossomed. He seemed to be turned in on himself.

JULIEN: Sly, yes. He always does things on the quiet. With the help of your son, incidentally.

TOUTE BELLE: I bring my son up in my way and he does very well.

JULIEN: So much the better for you, Madame.

TOUTE BELLE (*going toward the door*): I don't see that there is anything else to add.

JULIEN: Since you won't say anything to me, I'll go straight to the police station to report his disappearance.

TOUTE BELLE: We reap what we have sown!

Julien exits, furious. The boys come down the stairs laughing, and all three burst out laughing.

M. Bigey's room. Daytime. He is making notes, a racing sheet in his hands.

RADIO REPORTER: In the Golden Buttons Stakes, Fée Mélusine seems to have an excellent chance if the track doesn't get any slower . . . The First Step Stakes will bring out some thoroughbred one-year olds. Judging by the qualities shown in their trials, we prefer Persona Grata 506 and Petite Touche 512, in that order. Finally, the de la Fouilleuse Handicap has a very strong field, from which we select the top-weight Baba au Rhum 701, who is a first-class performer over the distance, and the long shot Whisky à Gogo 715, who has a good weight advantage.

ANNOUNCER: You have just heard the inside racing tips from Jean Varange. And now a communiqué from the Family Service Bureau, Ministry of the Interior, 11 rue des Saussaies . . . Antoine Loinod, thirteen and a half, left his home in Paris on November 18. Description: brown hair, brown eyes, small, active. He was wearing a gray and blue herringbone jacket, well worn, a checked woolen scarf, and corduroy slacks. If found, notify the Ninth Arrondissement Police or the Family Service Bureau, Anjou 28–30, Extension 835.

M. Bigey turns the set off.

M. BIGEY: René!

RENÉ (*off*): Papa.

M. Bigey paces up and down in the room and takes some papers out of a drawer as René enters.

M. BIGEY: This farce has got to stop.

RENÉ: What, Papa?

M. BIGEY: Point one. I didn't sign this report card; someone else did.

RENÉ: I didn't want to annoy you with such miserable marks. You have enough troubles, with Toute Belle, who doesn't want to sign that paper.

M. BIGEY: That has nothing to do with it. And anyway, if you had been a little more skillful . . . as skillful for instance as you were in getting up this letter to your principal imitating my handwriting, she would have signed the paper.

RENÉ: She wouldn't hear of it.

M. BIGEY: I learn from this letter that I have taken you out of school. Let's be consistent: I'll find a job for you.

RENÉ: That's logical.

M. BIGEY: Last point. I've had enough of the disorder due to the presence of your clandestine lodger.

RENÉ: But, Papa . . .

M. BIGEY: You thought you had me fooled. All those cigars, all those bottles that vanished, (*he takes the horse off the mantelpiece*) Star of Aran broken, patched up in this ridiculous way . . . That's the end of all that. Now the police are looking for him, and I don't want them in this house. I came up against them at a time when it was perfectly honorable; you'll understand that later. Today it won't do. Now, if that boy isn't out of here tonight, I'm sorry, I'll have to turn him in myself.

Daytime. Facing a square. Swings in background. Children playing.

RENÉ: The thing is to know what you want.

ANTOINE: There's a good one at my father's office.

RENÉ: Then you can't get scared.

ANTOINE: Do you want to do it?

RENÉ: I don't know the layout.

ANTOINE: But you know cops.

RENÉ: I know dough.

ANTOINE: *If* you can sell it.

RENÉ: You know pawnshops.

ANTOINE: Oh! Great!

RENÉ: You know how to hitchhike to the country?

ANTOINE: No. To the seashore.

RENÉ: Why?

ANTOINE: Because I don't know the sea.

11. This scene followed shot 290 in the original screenplay.

Loinod apartment. Evening. Julien hangs up the phone.

JULIEN: Now some more trouble! What a day! Gilberte! . . . I have to go out again.

Enter Gilberte, dressed to go out.

GILBERTE: So do I.

JULIEN (*sarcastically*): That's just fine . . . Well,
maybe we'll see each other for dinner. Only please,
no more sardines.

12. This is the way the interview with the Psychologist—and an intervening scene—appeared in the
original screenplay.

*Psychologist's office. Daytime. She is young, rather
pretty, and wears glasses. She is nervous and lights
every cigarette from the stub of the previous one.*

PSYCHOLOGIST: Come in, don't be afraid. And above
all, don't get the idea you're taking an examina-
tion. Not at all. I only want us to get acquainted.
Your name is Antoine Loinod and you are thirteen
and a half, right? (*No answer.*) At least answer
yes or no.

ANTOINE (*inaudibly*): Yes.

PSYCHOLOGIST: To start, tell me what this picture
shows. Take a good look at it. Keep calm.

Picture of an old man pulling a hand cart, 1900.

ANTOINE (*off*): I don't know.

PSYCHOLOGIST: Is your eyesight normal?

ANTOINE: Yes.

PSYCHOLOGIST: Very good. Now this one.

*Picture of a heavy-weight man sitting on a bench
with a young girl.*

ANTOINE (*off*): I don't know.

PSYCHOLOGIST: Yes, you do know. You don't want to
stay in this office for hours.

ANTOINE: More misery.

PSYCHOLOGIST: Is that all?

ANTOINE: Yes.

PSYCHOLOGIST: Now, what does this third picture represent?

Picture of a prisoner.

ANTOINE (*after a very long time*): A delinquent.

Same place, a little later.

ANTOINE (*very fast*): 1/5/3/0/9/4

PSYCHOLOGIST: 8/7/3/5/0/6

ANTOINE: 8/7/3/5/0/6

PSYCHOLOGIST: 7/3/0/6/2/9/8

ANTOINE: 7/3/0/6/2/9/8

PSYCHOLOGIST: Very good, now here's a sentence for you to repeat. Listen carefully. (*Reads.*) The subway is cheaper than the omnibus . . . Pardon me, than the bus. I'll repeat: "The subway is cheaper than the bus. It only costs . . . (*The paper says* "two sous." *She makes the mental correction*) . . . twenty francs. It's funny in Paris to see women drivers at the wheels of their taxis."

A trace of a mocking smile from Antoine.

PSYCHOLOGIST (*who has noticed his smile*): Repeat.

ANTOINE: The subway is cheaper than the bus . . .

Antoine is drawing. The psychologist watches him attentively. He hands her his drawing, showing his father, his mother, and himself, or so one could imagine.

PSYCHOLOGIST: Thank you . . . Now I'm going to read you some stories. At the end of each story, I'll ask you to answer one question. Are you listening?

ANTOINE (*absently*): Yes.

PSYCHOLOGIST: "A father bird and a mother bird and their little bird are sleeping in their nest on a branch."

Antoine sees this in the form of an animated cartoon.

PSYCHOLOGIST (*off*): "But now there is a windstorm. It shakes the tree and the nest falls to the ground. The three birds are awakened suddenly. The father flies quickly up into a pine tree, the mother to another pine tree." What will the little bird do? He can fly a little already.

The camera travels over the Psychologist's face as she asks the question.

ANTOINE (*his eyes vague*): It gives him a chance to visit his friend.

PSYCHOLOGIST: Good. Another one. (*She looks through her papers.*) "A boy comes in from school—or a walk—and his mother says to him: 'Don't start your homework just yet; I have something to tell you.'" What is his mother going to say to him?

ANTOINE: Go to the store.

At a fortune teller's. Gilberte is sitting opposite her; the fortune teller holds her hand.

FORTUNE TELLER: . . . You are nervous. Be calm. Concentrate . . . You need a change, of course, you are not satisfied. But is this the right time to change?

GILBERTE: That's just what I came to find out.

FORTUNE TELLER: I see things clearing up, that's for sure.

GILBERTE (*happily*): Oh, really?

FORTUNE TELLER: But not just yet, oh no, you have to be able to wait. For the time being I still see difficulties. There are even bars somewhere, someone behind the bars.

GILBERTE: It's my son.

FORTUNE TELLER: That's not fatal. He'll come out of it very well, if you let his destiny work itself out.

GILBERTE: Now, how about this person . . . What do you think I ought to do?

FORTUNE TELLER (*asserting and asking, at the same time*): Financially, the situation isn't at all bad . . .

GILBERTE: You can say that again. It's not like my husband.

FORTUNE TELLER: That counts, to be sure. Only, does he really care for you?

GILBERTE: If I only knew!

FORTUNE TELLER: I see him as rather cynical.

GILBERTE: Aha!

FORTUNE TELLER: He wants to have a good time, but he's not serious.

GILBERTE: So you think that . . . my husband . . .

FORTUNE TELLER: Hold on to him, until things do clear up . . . I'll give you more advice then.

The Psychologist's office. Daytime.

PSYCHOLOGIST: But how did you know?

ANTOINE: I talked to René about it—he's my pal— and he told me to look in the family book. So one evening when there was nobody home, I looked.

PSYCHOLOGIST: And that was a shock to you?

ANTOINE: No.

PSYCHOLOGIST: What! You found out that your father . . . isn't your real father, and that didn't make any difference to you?

ANTOINE: I thought instead it was my mother that wasn't my real mother.

PSYCHOLOGIST: Why? . . . (*Pause.*) What do you mean?

He bursts into sobs.

13. This scene followed the interrogation in the original, preceding shot 364.

The front steps of the building. Daytime. Antoine comes out. He has obviously just been crying, but he tries to act tough.

FIRST BOY: Say, did she make you draw a tree?

SECOND BOY: Did you see her legs?

THIRD BOY: Did she offer you a cigarette to make you talk?

Shot of young delinquents lined up in the street, all wearing the same blue dungarees.

COMMENTARY: Antoine often wrote me, and more than once the tone of his letters made me ashamed I was free. (*Quoting:*) "When we happen to leave the place to go for an X-ray or something, we go crazy just seeing the road, a sidewalk, or a bus." And so one Sunday I decided to go to see him.

14. This is the end of the film as it appeared in the original script, instead of shots 391 and 392.

A country road outside an inn. Late afternoon. Antoine comes up to a truck and sees written on the back of it: Fourcroy sur Mer. *He walks around the truck. No one is up front; he climbs up in back and hides under the tarpaulins. The truck starts.*

Interior of the truck. Daytime. Antoine sees something that might well be the sea; yes, the truck is going along a road by the sea, which appears and disappears. At a turn, as the driver slows down, Antoine jumps off the moving truck and takes a rather hard fall on the ground.

On the beach. Daytime. Low tide. Antoine goes forward first at a run, then very slowly, toward the water line, with its small ripples. He stops only when the foam starts licking at the soles of his shoes. He raises one foot, crooks the other, moves back, advances, moves back again, stoops to pick up a shell.

The last image here, Antoine at the shore, becomes a still and fades slowly into another live action shot: Antoine and René walking in the streets of Paris (this is a shot of them playing hooky, which we

have already seen). As we hear the last words of the
commentary, this image also becomes a still, remind-
ing us that it has been taken by a street photographer.

COMMENTATOR: And so I got a letter from Fourcroy
    sur Mer, and there I succeeded in seeing Antoine.
       How are we doing? Very well, thank you. And
    you? We are free and far from the tortures of
    adolescence, but when we walk along the streets
    we cannot help seeing as accomplices our suc-
    cessors in the third grade, as they begin their *400
    Blows!*

About *The 400 Blows*

ANDRÉ BAZIN

André Bazin nous a quitté le 11 novembre. Au mal implacable, il faisait face depuis cinq années avec une force d'âme exceptionnelle. Nous l'aimions et nous l'admirions sans réserve. La blessure que sa mort ouvre au flanc de notre équipe, rien ne pourra la refermer. Sans lui la critique n'aurait pas été pour nous un métier que l'on peut être fier d'exercer, sans lui le cinéma n'aurait pas évolué de la même façon. « Il a été le fil d'Ariane, écrit Jean Renoir, sans lui la dispersion eût été complète. »

Le présent numéro des « Cahiers » a été élaboré, préparé et rédigé avec lui : fait de son vivant, nous n'y changeons rien. Nous consacrerons à notre ami notre prochain numéro.

A sa femme, à son fils, à ses parents nous disons notre affection et notre fidélité.

LES CAHIERS DU CINEMA.

A Collage
from *Cahiers du Cinema*

1959 was a miraculous year for French cinema, a year of revolution and rebirth, but its beginning was clouded by the death of the nouvelle vague's *chief theoretician. André Bazin died on November 11, 1958, the day after shooting began on* The 400 Blows.

As the film's dedication indicates and as subsequent pages attest, Bazin was an extraordinary influence on Truffaut. The December '58 issue of Cahiers du Cinéma *featured, facing the contents page, an ←— obituary notice written by Bazin's fellow editors-in-chief, Jacques Doniol-Valcroze and Eric Rohmer.*

This same issue, which Bazin conceived and had completed editing before his death, included among other things a conversation about television between Bazin and Truffaut's co-scenarist, Marcel Moussy. But more than half the issue was devoted to a section called "Young French Cinema," which consisted of extracts from scenarios for films recently completed, in production or, hopefully, soon to be.

The 400 Blows *excerpt consisted of two scenes from the original scenario: what became shots 109-111 (pp. 48-50) plus the omitted scene 3 (page 163).*

True to their promise, the editors devoted their next number, "Noel," to "our friend," Bazin. Truffaut's memoir, a tribute to his mentor which was written during the filming of The 400 Blows, *follows:*

IT WAS GOOD TO BE ALIVE

It was good to be alive before André Bazin died. I blushed with pride if in the course of a discussion he happened to show his approval of me, but I felt an even keener pleasure when he would contradict me. He was the "Just Man" that you liked to be judged by, and a father to me. Even his reprimands were precious to me, for they were proof of an affectionate interest that I had been deprived of as a child.

The most moving memory I have of our relations goes back to 1952. Having deserted from the army on the eve of my departure for Indochina (I had signed up as a volunteer for three years, so I was completely in the wrong), I was languishing in the prison of Dupleix Barracks in Paris, along with a handful of deserters from the French battalion in Korea. There were a dozen of us in a cell built for four; the August heat and the smell of urine emanating from an old tin can made the air unbreathable; we would take turns climbing up along the door to breathe the air coming through a window overlooking the courtyard. Hanging onto the bars, the privileged prisoner of the moment turned around and said: "Anyone here named Truffaut?" I turned over on my mattress and heard: "Come look; your parents are here asking for you." More dumbfounded than glad, I hoisted myself up along the door and saw not my parents but the

Bazins, Janine and André, who had been refused permission to visit me and had hit upon the idea of opening a window along a stairway and shouting my name.

Then, for six months of daily effort and complicated procedures, they plugged away at the task of getting me out of the army, and finally they managed it. A similar thing had happened three years previously, as a matter of fact, when André got me out of the Center for Delinquent Minors in Villejuif.

I am only one of the innumerable people André Bazin helped during his lifetime, but I am probably the one he helped the most. In any case, he was the one responsible for my having crossed the abyss that separates the film-nut from the filmmaker, and for my being happy and being able to make other people happy: *"I'm practically a grandparent,"* he wrote me recently, having learned that my wife was expecting a baby.

Bazin got me to like Jean Renoir, and then to know him. I remember my first visit to the Hotel Royal-Monceau: we waited in the foyer till Renoir had stopped talking on the telephone; we couldn't see him, just hear him, and through the open door we spied a large battered beige hat lying on a chair: *"Octave's hat,"* André murmured with a conspiratorial smile.*

Bazin was a most unusual human being because of his great intelligence, his kindness, his honesty, and his logic: he surprised you at first and then very soon he charmed you. He never changed his behavior to suit either a person or a place, he remained himself in every circumstance, and used the same vocabulary to talk to a university professor, a concierge, a starlet,

---

* A reference to the character Renoir played in his film *Rules of the Game*. The prison scene described above, transformed, opens *Stolen Kisses*, the sequel to *The 400 Blows.—Eds.*

a cop, or a priest. This sometimes resulted in dialogues of the deaf; how it used to amuse Doniol and Rivette and me when we'd be walking down the Champs-Elysées and Bazin would approach a policeman to ask him to explain a fine that he felt was unfair! It was quite rare for the cop, who'd be exasperated at first and then literally flabbergasted, not to be convinced by a line of argument as refined in its logic as one of Bazin's studies on Bresson's esthetics.

And Bazin in a restaurant, Bazin at the plumber's, Bazin in a car, Bazin in a Pullman, are so many comic and moral "little flowers"—for André, like the Brothers of Saint Francis, was both amusingly and pathetically kind.*

Nonetheless André was not one of those boring moral theoreticians who are said to make you feel better when you come in contact with them: quite the contrary. After having talked with André you felt *worse,* but you also felt terribly proud to know such a great guy, a kind of saint in a velvet cap. Getting bawled out by Bazin was a pleasure because he radiated such warmth once his indignation was aroused, which didn't happen too often; you didn't say "How wrong I am," but "How right he is, how marvelous he is!" . . .

What people did was less important to him than what they were. For this reason, if you attacked such and such a filmmaker, such and such a journalist in his presence, he would defend not the filmmaker or the journalist, but the man, in a plea on his behalf that was always generous and intelligent; he could sketch psychoanalytic portraits of people that were astonishingly accurate; he gave everybody a chance, and he could easily have been the best

---

* A reference to the Rossellini film, *The Flowers of Saint Francis,* sometimes mentioned by Truffaut as his favorite film.—*Eds.*

lawyer of his generation.

This art of living, this free and easy manner of his, were not innate traits. I think that André suffered quite a bit as an adolescent because of his timidity and his frailness. He had bitter memories of his stay in the army and his career as a teacher. It was because he had courageously learned to live himself that he thought that you could, that you should, help others. André remained a very modest man; he had known me as a youngster, and it was probably to give me confidence that he treated me like an adult and never used the familiar form of address with me. And yet, when I came from Paris to see him, even quite recently, I felt myself become a child again and I was almost tempted to prattle like a kid in the unconscious hope of finding the same tone for our relationship that we had once had, with me playing the role of the adolescent in terrible trouble and Bazin playing the role of the grown-up friend who would always get me out of the worst predicaments.

But that Monday night, a few hours before his death, he could no longer speak and was groaning softly. We changed the cold compresses on his forehead without his being able to tell us whether or not this gave him any relief. As his arm slipped down over the side of the bed, I took his burning-hot hand in the hope of calming him. André, deprived now of the power of speech, seemed as frail and unhappy as a sick child whom, for the first time, I could help.

He died a little later that night, the victim of an illness he had fought against for ten years with unbelievable courage and discipline.

François Truffaut
[# 91, January, '59]

This preceded eulogies in honor of Bazin by Bardem, Bresson, Buñuel, Cocteau, Fellini, Gance, Renoir and, among others, the head of the Cinémathèque Française, Henri Langlois—to whom nine years later Truffaut was to dedicate Stolen Kisses.

That issue also included a review by Claude Beylie of Truffaut's short film, Les Mistons *(which was released in the United States under the euphemistic title of* The Mischief Makers): *The review also discussed, under the Proustian title* "Le temps perdu," *two other fine short films,* Low and Koenig's City of Gold *and Jean Rouch's* Les Fils de l'Eau [Sons of the Water.] *And Jean-Luc Godard was responsible for the two-page presentation of George Franju's first feature film,* Le Tête Contre les Murs [Head Against the Wall]. *The rear cover carried this still from another "big" picture of the coming year.**

---

* This was also the year of the Cinémathèque de Belgique's "Confrontation"—a balloting for "The Best Films of All Time" which involved some 150 film historians. The tabulation produced this list: 1. *The Grand Illusion* (Renoir); 2. *The Gold Rush* (Chaplin); 3. *Potemkin* (Eisenstein); 4. *Earth* (Dovzhenko); 5. *The Last Laugh* (Murnau); 6. *Citizen Kane* (Welles); 7. *The Cabinet of Dr. Caligari* (Wiene); 8. *Mother* (Pudovkin); 9. *Bicycle Thief* (DeSica); 10. *Intolerance* (Griffith); 11. *Greed* (von Stroheim); 12. *Passion of Joan of Arc* (Dreyer).

Cahiers countered, in the Bazin memorial issue, with its own list—the "electors" including Bazin, Chabrol, Godard, and Truffaut (with only Bazin voting in both competitions). The results: 1. Murnau's *Sunrise;* 2. Renoir's *Rules of the Game;* 3. Rossellini's *Journey to Italy* [released in the United States as *Strangers*]; 4. Eisenstein's *Ivan the Terrible;* 5. Griffith's *The Birth of a Nation;* 6. Welles' *Confidential Report* (U.S. title, *Mr. Arkadin*); 7. Dreyer's *Ordet;* 8. Mizoguchi's *Ugetsu;* 9. Vigo's *L'Atalante;* 10. Stroheim's *The Wedding March;* 11. Hitchcock's *Under Capricorn;* 12. Chaplin's *Monsieur Verdoux.*

In a note the editors specified that their vote was based more upon the *auteur's* total work than upon individual films, and they added the showing of the next twelve directors, in order: 13. Ophuls; 14. Lang; 15. Hawks and Keaton; 17. Bergman; 18. Ray [Nicholas, apparently, not Satyajit]; 19. McLaren and Flaherty; 21. Buñuel and Clair; 23. Visconti and Dovzhenko.

CAHIERS DU CINEMA

NOËL 1958

PRIX DU NUMERO : 350 Frs.   N° 90 - DECEMBRE 1958

The next month, February, this production still and caption appeared under the heading "Photo of the Month," with text by Jean-Luc Godard.

François Truffaut directing *The 400 Blows* with Jacqueline Decae asking [the psychologist's] questions and Jean Rabier operating the camera.

With *The 400 Blows* François Truffaut enters the modern French film world as if he were entering the school we went to as children. Humiliated children out of Bernanos . . . Melville-Cocteau's *Enfants Terribles*. And Vigo's children, and Rossellini's—in short, Truffaut's children, an expression that will enter everyday language as soon as the film is released. People will soon speak of "Truffaut's children," just as they speak of Bengal Lancers, wild drivers, and film addicts. In *The 400 Blows*, the camera of the director of *Les Mistons* is again placed not at the eye level of adults, as with "Papa" Hawks, but at the eye level of children. And if one implies arrogance when one speaks of the hauteur of those over thirty, one implies pride when one speaks of the hauteur of those under sixteen. In short, *The 400 Blows* is the

196

proudest, stubbornest, most obstinate and, in the
final analysis, the freest film in the world. Morally
speaking. Esthetically, too. The dyaliscopic lenses
Henri Decae uses give us a real eyeful, as they did
in *Tarnished Angels*. The working script is lively and
airy in texture, like that of *Passions Juveniles*; the
dialogue and action biting, as in *Baby Face Nelson*.
The editing is delicate, as in *The Goddess*. A dia-
bolical preciousness is evidenced, as in *The Left
Handed Gun*. The keys of my electric typewriter are
not lining up these titles just by chance: they all
figure on the list of the ten best films of 1958 drawn
up by Truffaut. An attractive, charming family, with
which *The 400 Blows* will fit right in.* What should
we say to sum up? This: *The 400 Blows* is a film
signed Candor, Fast Pace, Art, Novelty, Cinema-
tography, Originality, Impertinence, Seriousness,
Tragedy, Freshness, Ubu-Roi, Fantasy, Ferocity,
Friendship, Universality, Tenderness.

Jean-Luc Godard
[#92, February, '59]

In May, the month of the Cannes Festival, and

---

* Truffaut's entire "Ten Best" list for 1958: 1. Welles'
Touch of Evil; 2. Visconti's *White Nights*; 3. Penn's *The
Left Handed Gun*; 4. Nakahira's *Passions Juveniles*; 5.
Bergman's *The Seventh Seal*; 6. Cromwell's *The Goddess*;
7. Sirk's *Tarnished Angels*; 8. Sternberg's *Jet Pilot*; 9.
Siegel's *Baby Face Nelson*; 10. Preminger's *Bonjour Tris-
tesse*.

Godard's list: 1. Mankiewicz's *The Quiet American*; 2.
Bergman's *Women's Dreams* [also released in the United
States as *Women*; original title, *Kvinnodrom*] 3. *Bonjour
Tristesse*; 4. Becker's *Modigliani of Montparnasse* [*Mont-
parnasse 19*]; 5. Astruc's *End of Desire* [*Une Vie*]; 6.
Anthony Mann's *Man of the West*; 7. *Touch of Evil*; 8.
Villiers' *The Girl in the River* [*L'Eau Vive*]; 9. *White
Nights*; 10. Carbonnaux' *Le Temps des Oeufs Durs* [The
Time of Hard-boiled Eggs].

Resnais' list: 1. Malle's *The Lovers*; 2. Antonioni's *Il
Grido*; 3. Wajda's *Kanal*. 4. Marker's *Lettre de Siberia*
[Letter from Siberia]; 5. *White Nights*; 6. Abbott and
Donen's *The Pajama Game*; 7. *Women's Dreams*; 8.
Touch of Evil; 9. Logan's *South Pacific*; 10. *End of Desire*.

prior to the first public showing of the film, this essay appeared:

ANTOINE'S WAY

Les Mistons was all right; *The 400 Blows* is better. From one film to the other, our friend François has made the decisive leap, the giant step toward maturity. It's obvious that he's not wasting his time.

With *The 400 Blows*, we return to our childhood as we would return to a house that had been abandoned since the war. Our childhood (even if it is first of all a question of F. T.'s childhood) means suffering the consequences of a stupid lie, and involves humiliation, the revelation of injustice, abortive attempts to escape—no, there is no "sheltered" childhood. Speaking of himself, he seems to be speaking of us, too: this is the sign of truth, and the reward of real classicism, which knows how to limit itself to its object, but suddenly sees this object cover the whole field of possibilities.

For reasons that might be guessed, autobiography is not a genre that is very widely used in films. But this should not surprise us as much as the serenity, the restraint, the evenness of voice with which a past that parallels his own so closely has been evoked here. The F. T. that I met, with Jean-Luc Godard, at the Parnasse at the end of '49 or at Froeschel's or the Minotaure, had already done his apprenticeship for *The 400 Blows;* I swear we talked more of cinema, of American films, of a Bogart movie being shown at the Moulin de la Chanson than we spoke about ourselves, or else we merely alluded to our personal lives: that was enough. Or a snapshot produced suddenly would reveal what F. T. looked like three years before, at a shooting gallery, dazzled by the lights, pale, a smaller-sized Hossein, with Robert Lachenay leaning against his shoulder; or would show the three ritual rows of schoolboys in a fossilized class photo.

This mixture of vagueness and sudden enlightenment came finally to seem like real recollections, real memories. I'm almost sure of that now, for I recognized or rediscovered everything on the screen . . .

I should like the reader to really see my point: this film is personal and autobiographical, but never immodest. There is no exhibitionism of any sort here; Even *prison* is beautiful, but with a different sort of beauty. F. T.'s strong point is that he never directly speaks of himself, but instead patiently dogs the footsteps of *another* young boy (who perhaps resembles him like a brother, but an objectified younger brother), yields to him, and humbly reconstructs from personal experience a reality which is equally objective, and which he then films with absolute respect. Such a method of filming has a very fine name (and too bad for F. T. if he doesn't know what it is): its name is Flaherty . . . [One example] of the truth that can be attained by this method, and of the truth of the film in and of itself, is the admirable scene with the lady psychologist—which would have been impossible, incidentally, under the outmoded methods of shooting that people go on insisting we keep . . . Here, the dialogue and the direction emerge with all the truthfulness of "live" shooting; the cinema thereby reinvents television, and television in turn consecrates it as cinema; there is no more room here for anything except the admirable last three shots, shots that are pure duration, perfect liberation.

The whole film mounts toward this moment, and little by little sloughs off time in order to rejoin duration: the idea of length and shortness that so haunts F. T. seems in the end to have hardly any meaning in his case; or perhaps on the contrary it was necessary to have such an obsession about length, about *temps morts* ["dead moments"], such an abundance of cuts, of jerks, of breaks that eventually he could get rid of the old clockwork time and rediscover real time, that of Mozartian jubilation (which Bresson seeks too desperately to ever recapture) . . . *The 400 Blows* also represents the triumph of simplicity.

Not from poverty, nor from a lack of invention, quite the contrary: but he who from the beginning places himself in the center of the circle, has no desperate need to seek to square it. The most precious thing about film, and the most fragile, is also what keeps disappearing day by day under the reign of "clever" filmmakers: a certain purity of gaze, an innocence of the camera which here seems never to have been lost at all. It is enough perhaps to believe that things are what they are to see them simply *exist* on the screen as they do in life; can this belief have been lost by others? But this eye and this train of thought opening on the very center of things represent the filmmaker's state of grace: to be inside cinema *from the outset,* master of the heart of a domain whose frontiers can then extend to infinity: and to this we give the name Renoir.

I might also stress the extraordinary tenderness with which F. T. speaks of cruelty, which can only be compared to the extraordinary gentleness with which Franju speaks of madness; here and there, an almost unbearable force results from the constant use of understatement, and the refusal of eloquence, of violence, of explanation, giving each image a pulse, an inner quiver, that makes its mark in a few brief flashes that gleam like a knife-blade. We could speak, quite properly, of Vigo, or of Rossellini, or even more pertinently still, of *Une Visite* or *Les Mistons.* In the long run, all these references don't mean very much, but we must hurry and make them while there's still time. I just wanted to say, as simply as possible, that there is now among us, not a gifted and promising beginner, but a genuine French filmmaker who equals the very greatest, and his name is François Truffaut.

Jacques Rivette
[#95, May '59]

This issue also noted in passing the Paris premiere of Sidney Meyers' extraordinary film on childhood, The Quiet One (1948).

The June issue, much of it devoted to coverage of the Festival, featured The 400 Blows on its front cover.

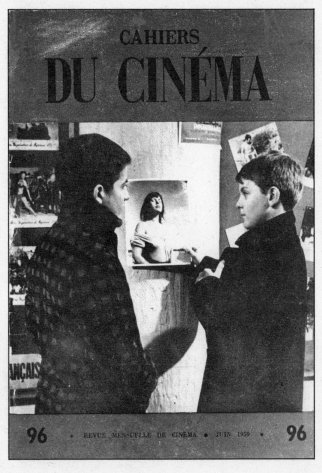

Overleaf there was this caption: "One begins by steal-
ing a cover of Cahiers du Cinéma, *and one ends up*
in the Cannes Festival."

In this context, these five variant or omitted scenes
from the original scenario are worth citing:

Outside. Carrefour Richelieu-Drouout, 10:00 A.M.

COMMENTATOR: For a long time in Paris, introductory
courses in how to play hooky have been given in a
darkened theater. Two boulevard moviehouses
opened at 10:00 A.M. and fortunately they faced
one another. So, from 9:30 on, a cluster of truant
schoolboys and schoolgirls kept watch, ready to run
from one sidewalk to the other. The first moviehouse to open got our business. And there, in this
atmosphere purified by the night and by DDT, ad-
venture began.

Inside moviehouse. Dialogue related to the film being
shown (heroism and violent justice). We see a bal-
loon of chewing gum emerge from René's mouth.

Outside moviehouse. Noon. Leaving moviehouse.

ANTOINE: Hey, look what's coming next week.

Suggestive picture of a scantily clad woman.

RENÉ: Yeah, but look at that.

He points to the notice: "For adults only."

ANTOINE *(contemptuous):* Oh, it's always that way.

COMMENTATOR: Since there was still some canteen
money left, we first sacrificed on necessities . . .

Antoine and René come out of a bakery and share a
loaf of French bread and a chocolate bar.

COMMENTATOR: . . . and then we moved on to essen-
tials.

At the pinball machines.

COMMENTATOR: The afternoon ahead of us still seemed enormous and Paris still full of surprises.

RENÉ *(to a passerby)*: Is this the way to the Eiffel Tower?

PASSERBY: No, you're going in the wrong direction. It's that way.

RENÉ: Thank you, sir.

René and Antoine then meet a peasant who's obviously overwhelmed by Paris, like a fish out of water. He explains to them that he has always wanted to go to the Eiffel Tower but has never managed to find it.

After dropping this last scene, and also a cab-ride scene with the boys still seeking the Eiffel Tower, Truffaut decided to use the traveling shots filmed for that sequence as backgrounds for the opening credits.

Also in the June issue was this "Notice from Cannes":

It says little to report that this picture was the high point and the justification of the Festival, the only other notable event being Buñuel's film,* and of course the admirable *Hiroshima Mon Amour,* which was shown out of competition.

Having exploded at the very beginning of the Festival, Truffaut's fireworks reverberated to the end, and the echo will continue to be heard long afterward. Two years ago, or even one year ago, *The 400 Blows* would have seemed like the anti-film of the festival, because of its author's personality and because of the film's style and the way it was produced. The fact that Truffaut is obliging some fifty traditional producers to ask themselves nervous ques-

---

* *Nazarín,* which won for Buñuel the Prix International.—*Eds.*

tions as they try to package similar films marks a milestone in the history of postwar French cinema . . . The proof provided by Chabrol should have been sufficient. *The 400 Blows* might then have been nothing more than disconcerting and the confirmation of our friend François' talent, had it not also been the rocket that burst right in the middle of the enemy camp and the one that marks its defeat from within. What makes it interesting that the explosion was felt in Cannes is the fact that distributors, advertisers, directors, technicians, actors, and officials were gathered together there in just the right quantity for the coup to be witnessed by the entire French film world, and to set them all to reflecting, with varying degrees of good faith. Each victory contains a potential revenge on the part of the vanquished, and it is possible that some day the tables will be turned as unexpectedly once again, but it is certain—and this is what is most important—that something new is about to begin, that the door that shook under the blows of Chabrol, Franju, Rouch, Reichenbach, and other fellows of their caliber (the door at which Astruc and even Vadim, let's not forget, were knocking quite a while ago) is about to give way, opening onto a new future.

This is what the evening of May 4 presaged, what we ought to thank Truffaut for, and what should give a feeling of pride to all those who believed in him and did everything in their power to get these explosive reels of film off to the south. Not the least of the paradoxes of this picture is the fact that the components of this explosion are gentleness, candor, and acute anxiety.

Bazin is dead. But Bazin lives, in effect, as posthumous producer of *The 400 Blows*. Were our comrade André still alive—and there is a lump in the throat at the thought of how overjoyed he would have been —this heartrending, joyous film about all the tenderness that exists in the world would naturally have been dedicated to Resnais.

Jacques Doniol-Valcroze
[#96, June, '59]

In July, Cahiers' "Council of Ten" cast its votes on the films which had opened in Paris during the previous month. →

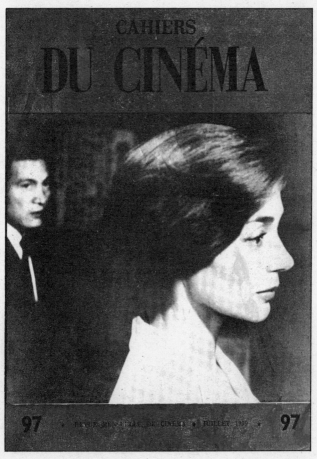

LE CONSEIL DES DIX

COTATIONS
- ● inutile de se déranger
- ★ à voir à la rigueur
- ★★ à voir
- ★★★ à voir absolument
- ★★★★ chefs-d'œuvre
- Case vide : abstention ou : pas vu.

TITRE DES FILMS \ LES DIX	Henri Agel	Jean de Baroncelli	Pierre Braunberger	Jacques Doniol-Valcroze	Jean Douchet	Jean-Luc Godard	Claude Mauriac	Jacques Rivette	Eric Rohmer	Georges Sadoul
Hiroshima mon amour (A. Resnais)	★★★	★★★	★★★★	★★★★	★★★★	★★★★	★★★	★★★	★★★	★★★
Les Quatre cents coups (F. Truffaut)	★★★	★★★	★★★★	★★★	★★★★	★★★★	★★★	★★★	★★★	★★★
Rio Bravo (H. Hawks)	★★★	★★★	★	★★	★★★	★★★	★★	★★★	★★★	★★★
Aventures fantastiques (K. Zeman)	★★★	★★★	★★	★★			★	★★	★★★	★★★
Comme un torrent (V. Minnelli)	★★				★★★	★★		★		★
Au milieu de la nuit (D. Mann)	★				★	★	★	★★	★★	
La Mouche noire (K. Neumann)	●		●							★
Les Chemins de la haute ville (J. Clayton)		★★	★	★	★	★	●	●		●
Prenez garde à la flotte (C. Walters)	●				★	●		★		●
Du Rififi chez les femmes (A. Joffé)	●	●			●	★	●	●		●
Le Génie du mal (R. Fleisher)	★	★	★	★				★		★
Chant de la Fleur rouge (G. Molander)	●		●	●		●	●	●		★
L'Enfer dans la ville (R. Castellani)		★						★		★
Le Bruit et la fureur (M. Ritt)	●				●			●		●

This issue, much of it devoted to a discussion of Hiroshima Mon Amour, *also contained a long review of the Truffaut film by Fereydoun Hoveyda, under the title "First Person Plural." In it he calls* The 400 Blows *(with* Hiroshima Mon Amour *) "one of the two most original films in postwar France." He ends with the hope that Truffaut will soon address us in the first person singular. (M. Hoveyda also prepared the Fiche Filmographique; #165, on* The 400 Blows *for L'Institut des Hautes Etudes Cinématographiques.) The number included, too, Jean-Luc Godard's review of the Cannes grand prize winner (Palme d'Or), Marcel Camus'* Black Orpheus.

In the August number, Godard's five-page treatment for A Woman is a Woman *was published.*

Two months later, in October, Doniol-Valcroze wrote seven pages on the ten-year history of Cahiers *(plus its three prior years as* La Revue du Cinéma*). In the midst of it he included these stills facing each other:*

François Truffaut in front of the boisterous schoolboys of *The 400 Blows* (background, center, Robert Lachenay).

Breathless: on opposite sides of the camera, Jean-Luc Godard and Jean Seberg.

Next month Truffaut's interview with Franju was featured. We have excerpted from the first four of fifteen pages, the rest of which are devoted to Franju's work. Franju, incidentally, before making the numerous short films that preceded his career as a feature film director, had in his youth started with Henri Langlois the collection of films and documents that were the basis for the Cinémathèque Française.

INTERVIEW WITH GEORGES FRANJU

[*From* Cahier's *introduction:*] Truffaut was busy staging and mixing *The 400 Blows* at the same time that Franju, on an adjacent set, was filming *Les Yeux sans Visage,* [released, truncated, in the United States as *The Horror Chamber of Dr. Faustus*] and when he could Truffaut visited him, so often that he says that *Les Yeux sans Visage* is the only film he ever made as an assistant learning the profession. Shortly afterwards Franju saw *The 400 Blows,* which made him as enthusiastic as Truffaut had been about *La Tête Contre les Murs* [*Head Against the Wall*] the winter before. This is why Truffaut and Franju talk a great deal about all three films in the course of this interview.

FRANJU: It appears that a prospective exhibitor fainted when he saw *Les Yeux sans Visage*. We should ask exhibitors not to faint, but even more important not to *cut* our films! Damn it all, *Grand Illusion* was cut in fourteen countries, and never twice in the same place. That's marvelous, because if they all cut the same things, you could say: they agree, so I'm the one who's wrong. But if they never cut the same things, they're the ones who are mistaken . . .

Joking aside, I was delighted with your film. Not just because it was you. No, I don't give much of a damn; I don't have respect for much of anything. But I was attracted by your stubborn persistence: first *Les Mistons*, then *The 400 Blows*, kids again . . . I must see it again; there are so many things in it. Everything is extraordinary, there's so much observation: the slap, the boy in the paddy wagon, the scene in the Rotor. And then the interrogation of the kid, filmed without a cut, it's great, *merde*. If you'd cut to the girl, the psychologist, it would have been stupid, it would have been ruined, it would have been completely traditional. That's what I call a *new* technique, because you kept focusing on his face without cutting. Haven't we been hounded about cutting back and forth, though? No, not cutting like that is much better—it's rare . . .

You'll see that people are going to talk about this sequence, I'm sure of it. This is the first film that ever showed a kid having a three-, four-minute conversation, with no cuts to anything else. As the person he's talking to isn't visible, he's speaking to the public, the brat, he's speaking to *us*. This confidence

209

is so moving, so new . . . I'm fascinated because there are so many people who bug you about rules and here it's so contrary to technique . . . It's unbelievably "incorrect", it's perfect, it really is! And you have a perfect right to do that. You're making a film dealing with reform schools, so you break cinematic rules, and it fits in with your film, with the tone of your film. You can't make a film against houses of correction using just "correct" techniques, now can you?

Everything those kids do, good or bad, is well done. You must never hide the camera with children. They're more instinctively aware than adults. With adults it's just the opposite—you have to creep up on their spontaneity, you have to lie down flat and hide. . . . But with kids it's not worth it to hide the camera, they are basically such good performers, they don't calculate their gestures, they don't compromise, they don't cheat, so why cheat with them? They don't know how to write, but they make very beautiful ink-blots . . . What really struck me was all the obsessive themes in *The 400 Blows:* garbage [*les ordures*], garbage everywhere, the kid is cornered between garbage cans, and then there're the eggs, and that Rotor . . . I don't see very many camera movements, but what there are are remarkable. The final traveling shot, with the kid running, is epic. This could be the end . . .

There is also a very fine pan shot, where the kid escapes from the camera as it pans, "running away" once again. And then afterward you catch up with him. These are the sorts of camera movements I like, ones that say something, that aren't made just to show the scenery or to be "cinematic."

TRUFFAUT: There is one shot I made with you in mind: the three little girls locked in the cage. Frankly, I thought of you: look, here's a shot for Franju . . . [see page 134]

FRANJU: It's terrifying. It's without a doubt the cruelest shot in the film, crueler than the slap. Caging those little girls—listen, that's monstrous. [*Laughter.*] What I also like very much is the story of the *Guide Michelin*. That's another obsessional theme. But you're full of them. Here's a guy whose wife is cheating on him. He doesn't notice, he's only aware of one thing: somebody's taken his *Guide Michelin*. Because it has to do with his job, he's a forwarding agent, obviously. It's a striking psychological and social insight. You rarely see anything that strong . . . I found the same thing in Lang. The *Guide Michelin!* The guy doesn't see that he's being cuckolded, he doesn't see anything that's going on around him: somebody's taken his *Guide Michelin,* but someone's also taken his wife. Now who could have a use for the *Guide Michelin*? The wife, and what for? To take a little trip with another guy, perhaps . . . No? That isn't it? That's what I imagined . . . It's too bad though . . . I said to myself: "She's gone off with a guy . . ." *Merde!* I thought I had it all figured out. I didn't see that it was the kid who'd swiped it . . . That's stupid . . . what a mistake.* It's really too bad . . . no, it isn't too bad at all! And then this guy always had banners and pennants around him; every time you see him, there are flags in the shot. The father's unbelievably fat-headed . . . and that dreadful woman . . . luckily there's the kid. He's outstanding, but they're all perfect. Decomble is admirable. And the boy's brilliant idea: "My mother? . . . She's dead!" Such a lack of respect commands respect. The boy is full of ideas . . . And suddenly the teacher almost embraces him. He's ready to whack him one, the boy's mother is dead, the guy suddenly becomes respectful—it's in-

---

* In his several subsequent revisions of the film—none final to date, it seems—M. Truffaut has restored in every case the scene with René from page 171.—*Eds.*

credible! What dupes adults are, though. It's the boy who knows what's true and what isn't.

TRUFFAUT: Let's talk about *Les Yeux sans Visage* ...

François Truffaut

[#104, February, '60]

Two months later, Godard's first feature, sponsored by Truffaut, has the cover: →

The month following, February '60, there appeared the Cahiers *"Ten Best" lists. Of these, we have selected ten:*

Claude Chabrol: 1. Lang's *Le Tigre d'Eschnapur* [joint title for two features, *Le Tigre du Bengale* and *Le Tombeau Hindou,* which were cut and combined in the United States release under the title *Journey to the Lost City*.], Mizoguchi's *Ugetsu,* Eisenstein's *Ivan the Terrible;* 4. Hitchcock's *Vertigo, The 400 Blows;* 6. *Hiroshima Mon Amour,* Hawks' *Rio Bravo;* 8. Mizoguchi's *Empress Yang Kwei Tsi* [*Yokihi,* released in the United States as *Most Noble Lady*.] 9. *Head Against the Wall;* 10. Stevens' *Diary of Anne Frank.*

Jacques Demy: 1. Bresson's *Pickpocket;* 2. *Ugetsu,* Varda's *Du côté de la Côte, Hiroshima Mon Amour, Ivan the Terrible,* Visconti's *Ossessione* [Obsession]; *The 400 Blows, Rio Bravo, Head Against the Wall, Vertigo.*

Jacques Doniol-Valcroze: 1. *Pickpocket;* 2. *Hiroshima Mon Amour;* 3. *Ivan the Terrible;* 4. *Ugetsu;* 5. *Vertigo;* 6. Bergman's *Wild Strawberries;* 7. *The 400 Blows;* 8. *Head Against the Wall;* 9. Rouch's *Moi un Noir* [I, a Black Man]; 10. Makovec's *Les Enfants Perdus* [in Czech, *Ztracenci;* literal translation, "The Lost Ones."]

Jean-Luc Godard: 1. *Pickpocket;* 2. Melville's *Deux Hommes dans Manhattan* [Two Men in Manhattan]; 3. Tazieff's *Les Rendez-vous du Diable* [working title for U. S. release, *Devil's Beast*]; 4. *Moi*

CAHIERS
DU CINÉMA

213

un Noir; 5. *Head Against the Wall,* Renoir's *Picnic on the Grass;* 7. *Hiroshima Mon Amour;* 8. *The 400 Blows;* 9. Chabrol's *The Cousins;* 10. *Du côté de la Côte.*

Jean-Pierre Melville: 1. Monicelli's *Big Deal on Madonna Street;* Minnelli's *Some Came Running;* 3. Preminger's *Anatomy of a Murder,* DeSica's *General Della Rovere, Hiroshima Mon Amour.* Vadim's *Les Liaisons Dangereuses. Pickpocket.* Robson's *Trial, The 400 Blows,* Bergman's *The Magician.*

Alain Resnais: (not in order of preference) Zeman's *Deadly Invention* [literal translation from the Czech, released in the United States as *The Fantastic World of Jules Verne.*] *Ugetsu; Wild Strawberries; Moi un Noir; Pickpocket; The 400 Blows; Rio Bravo; Head Against the Wall; Journey to the Lost City; Vertigo.*

Jacques Rivette: 1. *Most Noble Lady;* 2. *Ugetsu, Ivan the Terrible, Pickpocket;* 5. *Picnic on the Grass;* 6. *Anatomy of a Murder, The 400 Blows, Hiroshima Mon Amour;* 9. *Head Against the Wall;* 10. *Journey to the Lost City.*

Eric Rohmer: 1. *Ivan the Terrible;* 2. *Ugetsu;* 3. *Picnic on the Grass;* 4. *Rio Bravo;* 5. *Pickpocket;* 6. *Vertigo;* 7. *Wild Strawberries;* 8. *The Cousins;* 9. *The 400 Blows;* 10. *Hiroshima Mon Amour.*

François Truffaut: (not in order of preference) Bergman's *Brink of Life; Ugetsu; The Cousins; Picnic on the Grass; General Della Rovere; Hiroshima Mon Amour;* Fuller's *Run of the Arrow; Moi un Noir; Pickpocket; Head Against the Wall.*

Agnès Varda: 1. *Hiroshima Mon Amour;* 2. *Pickpocket;* 3. *Ugetsu;* 4. *Wild Strawberries;* 5. *The 400 Blows;* 6. *Moi un Noir;* 7. *The Cousins;* 8. *Vertigo;* 9. *Most Noble Lady;* 10. *Ossessione.*

Two Interviews

People
Michèle Manceaux

• *Because he made* The 400 Blows, *François Truffaut, the "young hoodlum," is representing France at Cannes.*

May 1958. A young critic who for five years has been preventing certain producers and directors from sleeping by attacking the cinema's most formally and officially recognized values is barred from the Cannes Festival.

May 1959. This same young man represents France at the Cannes Festival. His first film, *The 400 Blows,* has just been officially selected.

The story of François Truffaut could be told to tearful mothers and schoolchildren. He himself begins to tell us this story in his famous *400 Blows,* which he filmed for the same reason that people write: to free himself.

To a music that is rather lively, and as unconcerned as childhood (even the most unhappy one) is, the camera caresses the gray walls of Paris, stops in a school playground, enters a classroom, and surprises little Doinel standing in the corner with his face to the wall, scrawling. From this point on, the camera will desert him neither in his dreams nor in

From *L'Express*, April 23, 1959, reprinted by permission.

his wanderings—which grownups call, respectively, lies and running away. From the little apartment where his parents' nerves are constantly on edge to the house of correction within whose four walls he discovers life, other people, and the world, the camera will not leave him.

As Malle describes his environment, Vadim what he sees, Chabrol what he feels, Truffaut gives us his personal experience. The cinema of today's young directors has a literary ring to it. They are no longer out merely to shock us. Cinema has proved its technical possibilities. Now it must communicate. It has to have something to say. Truffaut, for his part, has a score to settle:

"I was born in Paris on February 6, 1932. I was immediately sent to a wet nurse, then handed over to my grandmother until I was eight. When my grandmother died, my parents took me back. They weren't bad people. Just nervous and busy. My father had only one thing on his mind: camping. My mother was embittered. No doubt she would have liked a more brilliant sort of life.

"In the film, the father thinks of nothing but cars, nothing but rallyes, and later the mother says to the judge about the child: 'He hates sports. He'd rather stay shut up for hours at the movies and ruin his eyes.'

"It's true that in my family there was something suspect about not liking the country; it was a sign of vice. My parents enrolled me at Rollin and then I flunked the exam to enter the upper grades. So they decided to send me to a local school.

"At this school there weren't any students who had come from the lycée. I was something of an outsider. At the lycée no one had played hooky. In this school it was an everyday occurrence. I started out by doing what the others did, and then I really acted up. The more I was punished, the more of a trouble-maker I became. So I was often expelled. I went from school to school, and I don't know how it happened, but I kept being placed in lower and lower grades. I once found myself in a class that I'd already been through three years earlier.

"I had a pal, Robert Lachenay, who is now a film critic and who was my assistant on *The 400 Blows*. We were always together, like the two boys in the film. We hid our briefcases behind the main entrance and streaked off to the movie theater with our lunch money instead of going to school.

"One day we'd skipped school so many times that we didn't dare go back. We said to ourselves: 'The more outlandish the excuse, the more likely people are to swallow it.' I went back to school and told the teacher: 'My father's been arrested by the Germans.' This was in 1943, and my uncle had been arrested the week before. There is always some element of truth in children's lies. But my father came to school to get me. This caused another scene, and I didn't dare go home.

"I was eleven years old. Lachenay told me that we could sleep in those subway stations farthest underground that had been turned into air-raid shelters. I went there. The shelter was swarming with people. They gave us a blanket, but they woke us at five in the morning to let the subway trains by.

"At this time people would give you a liter of wine for a quarter of a pound of copper, so we stole doorknobs or things like that, and sold the wine. My father found me, put me back in school, and told the school authorities everything I'd done. I was a black sheep. Everything I did was frowned upon, so I didn't go back. I used to go to the municipal library and devour Balzac.

"When the day of Liberation came, I was in a summer camp. The director sold the camp's food and we didn't have anything to eat. We were covered with boils and lice. We used to write out our complaints and the director said: 'I'm going to get you for libel.' We were very puzzled; we didn't know what 'libel' meant.

"Then they shaved our heads and I ran away. It was the first time I'd had my head shaved. I went back home then and tried to find work. I was fourteen.

"I applied for a job as stock boy at a seed exporter's. He soon was sorry he'd hired me. I didn't come to work very regularly. As soon as I got my pay, I went to the movies. After four months he fired me. It was Christmas. I'd gotten a bonus and with that and my severance pay I had quite a nice little nestegg. I went to live at Lachenay's and we decided to set up a film society at the Cluny-Palace on Sunday mornings. We bought a 16 mm print of *Metropolis* and named our club The Film Addicts' Club. But the screenings were terrible and people didn't come back. They went instead to Bazin's ciné-club at the Broadway, which also had its showings on Sunday morning. So I naïvely went to see André Bazin to ask him to change days. That's how we met each other.

"We talked about movies for a while, but a week later my father, who had discovered the announcement of The Film Addicts' Club in *L'Ecran français*, got his hands on me and turned me over to the police. The real article, not the juvenile authorities. I spent two nights in the central police station, as the boy does in my film. Then they locked me up in Villejuif.

"At that time—1948—Villejuif was half an insane asylum and half a house of correction. Delinquents who ran away were brought back by the asylum attendants. There were lots of young workmen there who'd swiped a few things, and young peasants who'd run away to see the big city. In my film, the main character is a city boy who wants to see the sea. He goes through the same process, and the process stops at this point.

"But life went on for me. I was saved by André Bazin. I wrote him and he went to no end of trouble to get me out. He went to see the psychologist and got me freed. My parents rather easily gave up the rights that, by law, they had over me. Incidentally, I wasn't unhappy at Villejuif. I was curious about everything. As I remember, we really weren't very wicked cases. When the guards were nasty, we used to invent very romantic excuses for them: 'It's because his daughter's got knocked up or his wife's left him.'

"Bazin finally got me out of there and found me a job at *Travail et Culture*.* I organized showings of 16 mm films in factories. But Bazin became ill and I was fired.

"I took a job in a welding shop; I earned sixty francs [approximately seventeen cents] an hour. I'd found something that was a lot of fun for me on Saturdays and Sundays. I went to the Club du Faubourg, and when there were lectures on movies, I would kick up a row. People used to laugh at how indignant I got.

"Then I fell in love with a girl. She and her mother sold yard goods in a shop. I went to live in a hotel just opposite the shop. I spied on her every night, but after a while I got tired of seeing her go to the movies with other guys, so I enlisted in the Army.

"After six months in the Army, they gave me a leave before going to Indochina. But I'd had enough of the army, and didn't go back. The trouble was,

---

* *Travail et Culture* [Work and Culture] was organized after World War II by veterans of the Resistance movement. Linked with the trade unions and subsidized by the government, it sponsored primarily lectures on cultural subjects. During its five-year life it involved the liveliest and most activist of the young intelligentsia. André Bazin played a prominent role in the organization. —*Eds*.

though, that I didn't have a penny to my name, no civilian clothes, and I didn't dare let Bazin know where I was.

"One night I happened to meet Chris Marker in a café. He was very surprised and said to me: 'I thought you were in Indochina.' So I told him the whole story. He telephoned Resnais and the two of them sent me off to Bazin's place in Bry-sur-Marne. Bazin persuaded me to turn myself in and go on sick call.

"I was sent to Villemain hospital. I smoked cotton and aspirin cigarettes so my heartbeat would go way up, but they decided to send me to Germany anyway. Some pals of mine had lent me some books. I wanted to give the books back before I left, and as I was returning them, I once again decided not to go back. But they came and got me and I left for Germany in handcuffs. They interlocked two pairs of handcuffs on me so that I could turn pages as I read. That made the soldiers laugh. I remember that I was reading the third issue of *Cahiers du Cinéma*, a great number on Bresson. Finally, at Kiel, they let me out for 'instability of character.' I think I deserved that description.

"I was twenty. Bazin gave me a chance to make my dream come true. I wrote a major article for *Cahiers*, an article opposing Aurenche and Bost. It went straight to the heart of the matter. After this article, I was asked to write one on film for *Arts*. I was earning twenty thousand francs [approximately fifty-six dollars] a month and things were going along nicely."

From this moment on, in fact, Truffaut knew what he was going to rebel against. With his friends from *Cahiers du Cinéma*, he formed an enthusiastic, reform-minded little clan that spoke of cinema as if it were a religion. There were exegetes and apostles. Truffaut went on a crusade, lashing out at some people and showering praise on others. Sickly looking, black-haired, with a pale complexion and the eyes of a sly child, he is not a man you warm to on first sight. He made many enemies. Hammer and tongs, he went after scenarists who are litterateurs and adapters:

In their minds, every story has characters A, B, C, and D. Within this equation, everything is organized according to criteria of which they alone have any knowledge. The scenes in bed are laid out carefully and symmetrically. Characters disappear, others are invented, the script departs from the original little by little and becomes a shapeless but brilliant whole. Infidelity does not rule out talent, but an adaptation is worth something only if it is made by someone familiar with film. These others want to add to cinema. They underestimate it. For them the director is the man who focuses the camera on their text.

For four years Truffaut and his friends Chabrol, Rivette, and Astruc defended the so-called *cinéma d'auteur*. Truffaut writes:

A film made by a team can be a fleeting success. It has an illusory homogeneity, but it doesn't hold up. Cinema cannot be an art so long as it is the result of the work of a group. Personal touches must replace the old, outworn tricks of the trade.

Renoir, Rossellini, Hitchcock, Bresson, Ophüls were their gods. Becker was in their good graces. When their admiration brimmed over, they came up with paragraphs like this:

Robert Aldrich is a *Cahiers* type of director. This means that he will be praised as often as possible, defended whenever necessary, and supported the first chance that comes our way.

Truffaut was the brilliant spokesman of the group that first praised Brigitte Bardot to the skies:

B.B. is the victim of a cabal. Chauvel* is the only person around who still thinks an actress is a lady who articulates better than others.

He didn't fear exaggerating and distributed praise and blame with equal passion.

Truffaut and his friends wanted to shatter everything, to revolutionize the cinema:

The cinema is going through a crisis because movies look like what the public expects. What is the value of an anti-bourgeois cinema made by the bourgeois and for the bourgeois?

And Truffaut cited well-known names: Allegret, Sigurd, Autant-Lara, Jeanson.

He was really a hateful *enfant terrible* who put his foot in his mouth with unbearable self-conceit. And to top it all off he was twenty-two years old. He said of Autant-Lara:

He is outrageous, he goes much too far. His film† is stupefyingly malicious. It is venom spat out as generously as hemoglobin. Hatred at times is a good counselor. Autant-Lara has made a successful film.

Autant-Lara replied by calling Truffaut "the young hoodlum of journalism." To this Truffaut answered: " 'Young hoodlum' is an outdated expression that leads straight to the Legion of Honor and a house in the country."

In May 1959, this seemed to have been borne out. Truffaut—who had railed against festivals in every tone of voice for three years in a row, who had exchanged registered letters with Monsieur Favre-Lebret, the director of the Cannes·Festival (letters in which the word "libel" was no longer meaningless

---

* The critic for *Le Figaro.—Eds.*
† *La Traversée de Paris* [*Two Bags Full*].*—Eds.*

to anyone)—was now the representative at Cannes of a country which is at least civilized enough not to bear a grudge.

A new school of cinema, born perhaps with the *Cahiers,* was about to compel recognition. According to Truffaut:

> Chabrol showed the way. After a short feature, *Les Mistons,* made with a tiny inheritance from Lachenay's grandmother, I was lucky enough to fall in love with and marry a girl whose father is a producer. He had confidence in me. My father-in-law helped me, it's quite true, but I would have made this film in any case. Film, after all, costs only fifty-seven francs a meter.* Rivette is filming right now with "short ends." Rohmer will shoot a film this summer with money from Chabrol's profits. They'll all make it.

Truffaut no longer had a sly look in his eye.

He repudiated none of his terrible criticisms, and especially not this one:

> Delannoy's *Chiens Perdus sans Collier* [*The Little Rebels*] is not simply a failure. It's an outright crime. We find here, in cleverly administered doses, various elements from *Jeux Interdits* [*Forbidden Games*], *Avant le Déluge* [Before the Deluge], *Los Olvidados* [*The Young and the Damned*], *Sciuscia* [*Shoeshine*], and even *La Strada,* watered down of course, vulgarized with all the stereotypes of the film for children: cheap cruelty, children who love each other, the little boy who admires the big one, the boy who's beaten, and so forth. The over-aged authors have forgotten how children talk.

Criticism is easy; art is difficult. Luckily for Truffaut, his child's heart is still alive. *The 400 Blows* is a cry from the heart.

---

* Approximately three and a half cents a foot.—*Eds.*

Truffaut: "The Young Cinema Doesn't Exist"
Interview with André Parinaud

François Truffaut has contributed to *Arts* for four years. His criticism, his ideas, his interviews, his surveys, the positions he has taken, the team of young journalists he has assembled around him, have helped to expose the formulas of the young cinema and have inspired vocations. We are happy to have welcomed him and proud to have supported him. (It is no mere lucky accident that *Arts* is the only weekly that regularly devotes a page to activities of the film world without any film company honoring us with its advertising, and it will also be recalled that last year the organizers of the Cannes Film Festival refused to invite François Truffaut, who nonetheless covered the activities of the Festival for our paper.)

In the area of film, as in that of theater or literature, *Arts* has continually fought to "disengage" the art of the image, the stage, and the pen from "management," and free it from pernicious influences. We are happy with the results, and they encourage us to pursue our efforts. For three years *Arts* has advocated a plan to reform the state-supported theaters—a plan which André Malraux has just put into effect. The new novel has found in our columns a discerning audience that is becoming more and more important. And now, following after Alexandre Astruc, Louis Malle, and Claude Chabrol, François Truffaut has just proved how valuable his ideas are in *The 400 Blows*. Other members of the film-page team will also present films soon. The fight for a new cinema will thus be pursued in the area of criticism, aided and abetted by concrete proof on the screen.

From *Arts,* April 29–May 5, 1959, reprinted by permission.

For the first time, François Truffaut, who has so often been on the interviewer's end of the microphone in our columns, now becomes the interviewee.

PARINAUD: In your opinion, are there common points, a certain technical or intellectual agreement, or at least shared tastes among young filmmakers? And can one really speak of the existence of a new cinematographic school?

TRUFFAUT: I see only one common point among young filmmakers; all of them quite systematically play the pinball machines, unlike the old directors, who prefer cards and whisky. This is not a paradox, because aside from this game, what I notice mostly is that there are essential differences between us. We know each other, of course, we like the same movies, we exchange ideas in a friendly way, but when the results of our work are judged on the screen, it is noticeable that Chabrol's films have nothing to do with Louis Malle's, which have nothing to do with mine. The films of the young directors bear an extraordinary resemblance to the people who make them, because they make them in complete freedom. And that's the only point we all agree on: freedom. The great French directors had long since lost the habit of choosing their subject—I mean an idea for a film that they bore within themselves, that they had in their guts and in their heads. When they became stars, the French directors came to be in very great demand. So they made their choices on the basis of the deals they were offered.

PARINAUD: Let's try, then, to define the young cinema in comparison with the old cinema.

TRUFFAUT: It seems to me, first of all, that the young directors are more preoccupied by what happens on the screen than by technique. They attach great importance to the characters and the subjects of their films. They have a greater respect for the public and the somewhat naïve idea that what interests them ought to interest movie-goers. They maintain that if the story pleases them, it will please others, and that their sincerity pays off. But there are no common esthetic approaches. There are only chance resemblances.

PARINAUD: Is it also due only to chance that in less than fifteen months five films by young directors have been made?

TRUFFAUT: Let no one get the idea that producers take an interest in young filmmakers. They're only interested in success. There is one point, if you wish, that young filmmakers have in common: they have found financial backing for their films outside the film industry, thanks to their family or their in-laws or an inheritance.

PARINAUD: What place can we say the young filmmakers' movement has in the history of cinema?

TRUFFAUT: It can be said, roughly, that cinema has gone through three stages: first, the silent era, when film was a physical performance, the era of Griffith and John Ford. Making a film in those days was like being in a wrestling match: the director bore the weight of a film, and a considerable amount of equipment, on his shoulders. He had to get a cast of thousands moving. The Deglane of this era—that is to say the wrestler at his purest—was Griffith, and the executioner of Béthune* was Cecil B. De Mille.

With the era of the talkies, cinema became more intellectual. It became a by-product of the novel, and above all of the theater. It fell into the hands of the

---

* Armand Louis de Bethune was an aristocrat guillotined during the French Revolution.—*Eds.*

semi-intellectual. This era was represented at its worst by the Feyder-Spaak duo and at its best by Prévert and Carné.

We have now entered the third stage: that of the intellectuals, an era when physical performance no longer enters the picture, when all the technical problems are taken care of by a large and experienced film crew. The technical procedures are now completely developed, and the film is ultra-sensitive. Proof that there are no longer any technical problems lies in the fact that our first films are as finished as the fifteenth film of this great director or that, whereas at one time this would have been impossible.

Cinema today is in the hands of intellectuals, that is to say, people who in other circumstances might have written novels or plays, and who a dozen years ago would doubtless have preferred to write novels or plays out of fear of the technical problems involved in making a film. We are in the age of author-cinema. An intellectual cinema runs the risk, of course, of very quickly becoming dry and abstract. But there is also more chance of its becoming intelligent, strong, and sincere than there was in earlier periods.

PARINAUD: So we shouldn't talk of revolution, but of evolution.

TRUFFAUT: Exactly. It's a question, for young filmmakers, of regaining the healthiness of the silent era, a marvelous state of health that is the one thing that can help our cinema avoid becoming tense, knotty, boring, and dry. We must rediscover the freshness of the first era of cinema and deny absolutely all of the second era, which can be seen today to have been a transitional stage.

PARINAUD: In your opinion, who are the most despicable dialogue writers and scenarists in this second period, those who contributed most to ruining cinema's health and those whose influence remains the most dangerous?

TRUFFAUT: Aside from the three names that dominated the prewar cinema, that is, Renoir, Gance, and Jean Vigo, the screen was only a by-product of the theater and the novel. Charles Spaak seems to me the most compromised man of that era. I would also mention Jeanson, who popularized the style of the Boulevard theater. When Jeanson states that he is fighting the cult of the director by claiming that the real author of a film is the dialogue writer, he's right, because all the films he wrote were shot by men who took a back seat to him, who had nothing to say, so that he really was the "author" of these films. But if I were in his place, I wouldn't boast about it.

PARINAUD: If one cannot define the formula of the young cinema, perhaps one can define the intellectuals who have created it.

TRUFFAUT: First of all, they're people who aren't afraid. They aren't at all afraid to talk things over with producers. The young filmmakers make it a point of honor to be good businessmen. They are absolutely free of the old notion that money is against art or the film industry is against art in the cinema. They want to reconcile art and money instead of setting the one against the other. There is always the danger, of course, that success will oblige them to work according to the usual standards. They risk being sought out very soon by producers who say: "You've made your film with thirty million francs; we'll give you a hundred twenty for your next one. You'll see how much simpler everything is." Yes, the danger is the second or third film.

PARINAUD: What is your position on that subject?

TRUFFAUT: There are only particular cases. It is obvious that you can make three cheap films and still hanker to make an expensive film. It can also be useful to use certain stars. The problem is to safeguard your freedom as much as you can.

PARINAUD: Did the fact that you made your films completely independently with whatever means were at hand contribute anything new to your work?

TRUFFAUT: Certainly. Where an experienced director would shoot fifteen takes, we shot only one or two. This stimulated the actors—they knew that we wouldn't redo things, so they just dove in. Thus our images don't have the icy perfection so common in French films, and the public was touched by the spontaneity of our work.

PARINAUD: But this is something that happened by chance, something to do with a lack of polish, if I understand correctly.

TRUFFAUT: Absolutely. And this is already something in the world of film. It gives films an external truth that has its own importance. For example, in ordinary films, when a scene is made with the characters talking inside a car, you film it in a studio by process shots: you project images made previously by the cameraman and they flash by outside the windows of the car. It's very noticeable that the actor isn't driving, that he's reciting his lines without watching where he's going. All the automobile-drivers in the audience wonder why the car doesn't hit a tree. Because we couldn't afford process shots for such a scene, we attached the camera to the front of the car, the first time this had been done for years and years. As a result, we obtained a more lifelike scene. The streets were real, what the actor did was real, and this scene moved the audience. But this gimmick that circumstances forced us to use must not become a systematic thing.

Anyway, you obtain a profound truth through creating a surface truth—and sophisticated cinema had lost even this superficial truth. The actors' clothes, for instance, were never wrinkled, and people's hair was never mussed.

PARINAUD: You speak of a lack of financial means, yet you filmed *The 400 Blows* in CinemaScope.

TRUFFAUT: But CinemaScope isn't a luxury. The only extra cost is renting a special lens, which comes to about a million francs per film. On the other hand, it allows you to save quite a bit of money by shooting longer and fewer sequences. Moreover, by using 'Scope I obtained an indispensable effect. The decor of my film is sad and shabby and I was afraid it would become a distasteful background. Thanks to 'Scope, I obtained a stylistic effect by taking a broader view. Thus, at one point, my character goes out to empty the garbage. Thanks to 'Scope, the scene seems less sordid than it would have appeared in a normal-sized image. Yet it remains quite realistic. In the same fashion, my film could end on neither an optimistic nor a pessimistic note. I avoided solving the problem by dramatizing it. Instead I took advantage of the large screen and froze the image of my hero, whose face becomes motionless, with the ocean as a background.

PARINAUD: It seems to me that most young film-makers who have just come before the public have one thing in common. They are all students, or at least constant customers, of the Cinémathèques. They did not learn their trade behind the cameras, but rather by seeing films.

TRUFFAUT: At one time people came to the world of film by accident. Today, it's quite true that people want to make films because they've seen films and loved them. They no longer go to movies by chance, but rather with the firm intention of making films.

In my own case, I was twelve when I decided to be a film director because I'd been seeing movies.

Obviously these conditions give rise to the risk that no one will try to re-invent cinema, as should be done, but only to copy it. This is where temperament can enter into the picture.

PARINAUD: Did young directors digest the education they acquired in the Cinémathèques? Aren't they in the same position as certain teachers of literature who were once preparing for the Ecole Normale, who come to the novel marked a little too deeply by the history of literature? Don't they risk imitating too much rather than inventing?

TRUFFAUT: In my opinion, this education is no handicap. It's even progress compared to the preceding generations where you got to be a director by working as an assistant. The assistants imitated their bosses' way of doing things, and not the classics. Which led to the style that you might call "French cinema"—artificially elegant, horribly monotonous, and quite inferior to the flexibility of American movies.

Since you want some definition of the young cinema, let's say that we all come to the screen by detesting French cinema and admiring the Americans, whose free and easy manner where technique is concerned and whose flexible camera we have kept. Of course, so far as our creative resources are concerned, our heritage is French.

PARINAUD: Can it be said that the young filmmakers are ambitiously seeking to contribute something new through their ideas about dialogue?

TRUFFAUT: Negatively, yes, insofar as we disapprove of dialogue à la Audiard or Jeanson, who present only witty persons who can sum up their experience in felicitous, brilliant aphorisms, down to the very last little phrase. Or the dairy-maid who speaks as forcefully as an engineer, passing final judgment on the fate of the world and life. We want to capture truth. We are attempting to make the dialogue less theatrical.

My dialogue writer for *The 400 Blows,* Marcel Moussy, has played a crucial role in this respect. I called on him after having seen his television program: *If It Were You.** He's extremely good at writing dialogue about family conflicts, and his experience as a teacher has inspired him to write pupil-teacher dialogue that strikes everybody because it's so true to life.

The same is true about the choice of subject matter. We make films where almost nothing happens. Neither blood nor fisticuffs, nor big scenes, nor violence, just a succession of little everyday incidents that go to make up the fabric of the film. The danger, of course, is that you might create a new fashion or take to watching yourself too closely.

PARINAUD: You are going to be faced with a problem soon: the star problem. How can it be resolved?

TRUFFAUT: Personally, I shall consistently refuse to make films with these five stars: Fernandel, Michèle Morgan, Jean Gabin, Gérard Philippe, and Pierre Fresnay. They're artists who are too dangerous; they decide on the scenario or make changes in it if it doesn't please them. They don't hesitate to inflict an entire cast upon you or to reject certain actors. They influence the direction, and they demand close-ups. They do not hesitate to sacrifice the best interests of a picture to what they call their "image," and in my opinion they are responsible for numerous failures. I am happy to have made this statement, because

* Moussy's "program" by this title was a series of ninety-minute dramas based on fact.—*Eds*.

this way I'll run less risk of giving in to temptation. But fortunately cinema doesn't rest on these five heads. It's even been proven, as we have seen recently, that these stars sometimes fail at the box office. But there are intelligent actors and actresses— I might mention Jeanne Moreau, for instance, who is well known for her flexibility and her kindness; she doesn't even want to be shown the rushes so as not to have hasty impressions of her acting. It would be ridiculous not to accept the collaboration of artists of this sort.

PARINAUD: Why did you choose the experience of adolescence as your first film subject?

TRUFFAUT: The subject had been on my mind for a long, long time. I first tried making a short subject, called *La Fugue d'Antoine* [*Antoine Runs Away*]. Then little by little the film came to be a sort of chronicle of adolescence, and more particularly the age of thirteen, which is the most difficult to get through. I chose this subject for my first film because I'm more at ease with children than with adults. And naturally I'm more at ease too when I paint a situation that I went through myself not so long ago. Finally, adolescence is a subject that has rarely been explored in films, and one that's rich in possibilities.

The 400 Blows is not an autobiographical film, but I was inspired by certain circumstances in my life . . .*

I could have chosen another subject and used my memories or thoughts in the same way. I wanted most of all to paint a portrait, the most accurate portrait possible, of a particular time during adoles-

---

* Here M. Truffaut recounts the experiences told in the *L'Express* interview, pp. 215–223, implying that this interviewer hired him for *Arts* after having read the article on Aurenche and Bost. He further remarks of his personal experiences that he transposed them for the film. —*Eds.*

cence—that is to say, a moment teachers and sociologists are quite familiar with, but which parents generally don't know about—and the existence of which they apparently don't even suspect. I made my film on this crisis that specialists call by the nice name of "juvenile identity crisis," which shows up in the form of four precise disturbances: the onset of puberty, an emotional weaning on the part of the parents, a desire for independence, and an inferiority complex. Each one of these four factors leads to revolt and the discovery that a certain sort of injustice exists. I didn't amuse myself by systematically illustrating these attitudes, but I believe that a psychologist could easily find them if he analyzed my film.

PARINAUD: How did you choose the youngsters in your cast?

TRUFFAUT: By little ads. Of the hundred or so kids who showed up, I chose forty, and immediately noticed Jean-Pierre Léaud. I can say of him that he not only was the character just as I had imagined him, but that his health, his spirit, his muscle tone made my film better. I had imagined my character as being more delicate and more timid. He gave the character greater freedom.

PARINAUD: What lesson have you drawn from this first film? Have you changed certain of your critical opinions?

TRUFFAUT: I have become more indulgent—that is to say, I have lost all intention of reforming cinema. Bad films don't make me indignant the way they once did. I only want to make good films. I've lost a little of my purity as a lover of film. I have become selfish like all directors. I try to fight against this tendency, and I'm somewhat afraid of the future.

PARINAUD: What, in your opinion, is the most important thing that's happening in the world of film today?

TRUFFAUT: I think that people are wrong to speak of a takeover by new directors. There are only a few arrivals, and no departures. On the other hand, there should be more interest in young scenarists. That's what's really happening. Jean-Charles Pichon, with *La Tête Contre les Murs,* Pierre Gascar with *Les Yeux Sans Visage,* Louis Sapin with *Les Dragueurs* [*The Chasers*], Louise de Vilmorin with *Les Amants,* Marcel Moussy, Paul Gegauff—that's where the real takeover is happening. These are the people who are going to set a style, who'll change the old tricks of the trade.

I once wrote an article in *Arts* on the critical state the French cinema had reached concerning ambitiousness. I wrote that in literature eighty per cent of the novelists aspire to the Prix Goncourt, but there weren't three filmmakers a year who wanted to win the Prix Delluc. With the young filmmakers this is changing. Whether they're successful or not, all the films we make are ambitious. And this is very important. You can talk for hours about whether a film is good or bad, but you realize very early on that it's an ambitious film. This ambitiousness might perhaps be the basis for helping cinema. The premium placed on quality should reinforce filmmakers' intentions— that is to say, their ambition. We must hope that shortly hereafter the jury for the Prix Delluc will have submissions by thirty directors instead of three or four. That it will have only an embarrassment of riches to choose from. That's when French cinema will be saved.

Four Critics

The Importance of Subject Matter
Georges Sadoul

The hero of *The 400 Blows* is a young boy (Jean-Pierre Léaud, thirteen years old) who lives in the Pigalle section of Paris. Do his parents love him? They don't understand him, because they lack affection or lack time. The husband (Albert Rémy) is a white-collar worker, very proud of his car and of being the secretary of an automobile club. The wife (Claire Maurier) is a part-time secretary. She looks down on her husband, who is the legal father, but not the real father, of her son. She has lovers.

The family lives in a tiny apartment. The boy's bed is made up every night in the entryway, and the three of them must step over it to go in or out. The apartment is on the sixth floor and there is no elevator. The boy goes down a dark, peeling staircase to take out the garbage.

He isn't much happier at school than he is at home. The teacher (Guy Decomble) doesn't like this inattentive, daydreaming child. Late to school because of his parents, the boy decides to play hooky with his best friend (Patrick Auffray). They loiter around the neighborhood. At the Clichy subway entrance,

From *Les Lettres Françaises*, No. 777, June 11, 1959, reprinted by permission.

the boy sees his mother being kissed by a man who is not her husband.

The next day, needing an excuse for being absent, the boy tells the teacher that his mother has just died. He is pitied and consoled—until his mother, alerted by a little informer, arrives at the school, very much alive.

After this scandal, the boy neither wants nor dares to go back home to his parents. He sleeps in a printing plant and wanders through the streets of the neighborhood. He returns to school. His father comes to get him there. Family life begins once again. For a French composition: "Tell the story of the death of an old man," the boy finds a passage in Balzac's *La Recherche de l'Absolu* [*The Search for the Absolute*] and copies it. Out of gratitude, he sets up an altar to Balzac. A lighted candle sets fire to the altar. The parents soon forgive him and the whole family goes off to spend a happy evening at the Gaumont-Palace.

The teacher recognizes Balzac's prose. He expels the boy, who flees the school and his family. His friend hides him in the ramshackle studio where his father (Georges Flamant) lives. Swiping things here and there, they dream of going to the ocean. To get money for the trip, the boy takes a typewriter from the office where his father works. He can't pawn it, and when he goes to put it back in the office he is taken by surprise and held prisoner by the janitor of the building.

His father turns him over to the police. He is locked up in the local police station with prostitutes and pickpockets. Then come the paddy wagon, the central police station, fingerprinting, photographing, a prison cell . . .

At his parents' request, the boy is sent to an observation center for minor delinquents, a modern version of a reformatory. He can see his mother, who is more bitter than ever, but he can't see his pal. Life in prison is hard. He escapes into the Normandy countryside.

"As he runs through the fields and the prairies, he finally reaches the ocean, which he has never seen. Reconciled with nature, will he soon be reconciled with life?" This is the way the scenario ends in a resumé of it that very likely was written by its author.

The conference at La Napoule last month brought several directors together, among them François Truffaut. The final report declared in substance that the participants had found themselves in agreement on essential points but could agree on none of the details.

As for these essential principles, the youngest participant in the conference, [Jean-Daniel] Pollet, apparently wanted some sort of motion on subject-matter and content to be included. "It is obvious that what brings us together is the fact that the subject-matter is of no importance to us," he reiterated in several ways, according to the report published in *Arts*.

This peremptory, juvenile statement appears not to have been accepted by anyone; quite the contrary.

The fact is that to give an account of the first Truffaut film (and yesterday of Chabrol's two and tomorrow of Alain Resnais' first), the critic must first tell the story in detail, because it is more important than the way the shots are set up or the way the camera moves. This does not mean that these films don't have a style, but rather that it remains subordinate to the content.

"For recent directors the subject-matter is very important," one is tempted to write, taking the opposite position from Pollet. This has been proven to us

238

by a *reductio ad absurdum*. Those under thirty (or forty) who, willy-nilly, have dealt with traditional, accepted, or superficial subjects have not yet made their mark where art is concerned: for instance, Molinaro and *Un Témoin dans la Ville* [*A Witness in the City*], Robert Hossein and *Toi, le Venin* [*Nude in a White Car*], Boisrond, and to a certain extent Pierre Kast.

It is certain that the subject-matter of *The 400 Blows* lay close to François Truffaut's heart. As everybody knows, his film told of the beginning of his own adolescence, closely following what really happened in almost every detail. No doubt Truffaut didn't steal a typewriter and instead was put in prison because of his imprudent management of a film society. This is a legitimate transposition. And those who saw Truffaut and Jeanne-Pierre Léaud at Cannes certainly didn't see a director showing off his star. Nor were the two of them father and son, or two brothers, one older and one younger. What they saw was a creator and his young self-portrait—himself "as a Young Man," to borrow a title from James Joyce.

One autobiography naturally leads to the citing of others. *Zéro de Conduite* [*Zero for Conduct*] has often been mentioned in connection with *The 400 Blows*. The relationship seems to me to be limited to the genre and the subject-matter. Truffaut's tone and style bear little resemblance to Vigo's. There is a closer resemblance to *Premières Armes* [*First Arms*], in which René Wheeler also told of the end of his childhood, in a film in which Guy Decomble was a character much like the bookstore man in *Les Cousins* and the professor of *The 400 Blows*. This book reminds one above all of a book that François Truffaut probably is not familiar with, Jules Vallès' *L'Enfant* [*The Child*].

Since the question of pessimism is often posed (either well or badly), I will say that the film is much less "black" than the novel I have mentioned —on condition, of course, that the book is taken in and by itself, forgetting the fact that this autobiography is part of a trilogy, of which *L'Insurgé* [The Insurgent] and the revolutionary battles of the Commune are the logical conclusion. But the asphyxia of a child is more stifling during the 1840's in Vallès than during the 1940's in the cinema.

Truffaut and his collaborator Marcel Moussy have not created a universe where everything is black and white, where children are persecuted angels and the "grownups" heartless, ruthless monsters.

The parents are not monstrous, but human, because their feelings (good or bad) are not prefabricated. We blame them, certainly, but we also pity them because their cruelty is not an inherent, inborn fault, a curse of the Creator, but the result of definite and particular social conditions.

The father goes very naturally, with no malice, to the police to ask them to arrest his son. He thinks that this is "what is done" in such a case: when a child has stolen, one "goes to the police," as one "calls a doctor" when a child has whooping cough. After all, "difficult children" need character training in the right institution.

The father and the mother are prisoners of a "way of life." They are petty bourgeois, no worse than many others. Their social status determines their conception of the world. The "punishment" they inflict on their child matches their furniture, their pleasures, and their tastes perfectly. Everything about this man fits together: his gossip about the office, his car, his ambition to hold an important office in an automobile club.

Yet they are not "evil people." Above and beyond

their personal failings, the father and mother are victims of niggardliness and pettiness—both in the way they live and the way they think. When both of them work, there is hardly any free time left. If it is taken up by quarrels, troubles, bitterness, what is left for their young son? At the end of *The 400 Blows,* the child judges and characterizes his parents, with insight and without any malice or rancor. After all, they have loved him in their own way, and he owes a few good moments in his life to them. The evening, for instance, when the tragedy that the fire in the Balzac shrine might have brought on suddenly turns into a comedy, a party marked by wholehearted trust and affection.

It is evident that the universe of *The 400 Blows* is very far removed from that of the *films noirs*—of the type of *Une Si Jolie Petite Plague* [A Rather Pretty Little Beach]*—which were popular ten years ago in the French cinema.

Doubtless things are not all rosy in Truffaut's universe. But are they in our world? Is everything so perfect in contemporary society that it must be transformed into a pastoral? In the glorious French school of the years 1934–1940, "poetic realism" was always critical and very often bitter.

Truffaut goes back beyond our postwar cinema and claims kinship with the prewar era when he chooses Jean Renoir as his principal teacher and proclaims *La Marseillaise*—a film that was long a bone of contention and long disparaged because it directly expresses the spirit of an era—a "work of genius." And it is this director that this film harks back to, not to a Hitchcock or a Sacha Guitry (!!!),

---

* A film by Yves Allegret, starring Madeleine Robinson and Gérard Philippe (never released in the United States).—*Eds.*

whom Truffaut the young critic once praised to the skies out of personal taste for him or as an impertinent paradox.

If one compares the new French directors of 1958–1959 to those whose talent blossomed in 1935–1936, they may be deemed to be "backward" in the domain of social criticism. We shall comment further on this comparison someday. For now, let us merely note that there may be something arbitrary about it if we separate the art of the film from historical conditions (1935–1936 saw other events besides the rebirth of our cinema). And if we forget that Jean Renoir's *La Marseillaise* was not his first film but his twentieth, his *Fille de l'Eau* [Daughter of Water] or his *Petite Marchande d'Allumettes* [The Little Match Girl] or his *Charleston* at the end of the 1920's were further removed from contemporary reality than *The 400 Blows*.

"I am surprised myself at how much importance I attribute to giving some idea of the social background of my characters," François Truffaut said. This thought of his (whether he is conscious of it or not) goes beyond the choice of the cast or the writing of the scenario. The care he takes to situate his characters socially by their outward appearance, certainly, but also by their conversation, their behavior, their furniture, and so on (following the strictest Balzacian or "Jean Renoirian" methods) leads him to go beyond description to criticism. Who can claim that *The 400 Blows* is a film to the glory of French society under the Fifth Republic? Or say that it has nothing to do with the reality of our country?

If we run back over this film in our memory— that far-seeing critic who tends to remember the most successful parts best—it will remind us first of all of the agonizing scene at the police station, the caging of a child, the awkward indifference of the cops, the paddy wagon . . . Something more than rebellion comes through in such a scene.

The return to Renoir (especially the Renoir of the thirties) is accompanied by a fidelity to the neo-realist methods followed by Rossellini. An esthetic bias—much more than a dearth of funds—was responsible for the constant recourse to real-life (or sparsely furnished) interiors. If the question of neo-romanticism is brought up (there is as yet no certain answer to this question), Truffaut the neo-romantic dialectically follows the Italian neo-realism of 1946 as well as the French realism of 1936, though he parts company with them on certain points (rightly or wrongly).

Wanting to situate this film in our country and our time, we have talked too much about art, esthetics, influences, historical analogies. What matters most is that *The 400 Blows* has moved us profoundly by its conviction and its sincerity.

Violence in it is tenderness, and mournful reality is vibrant poetry . . . One understands these moving qualities better when one is still under the sway of the emotion the film generates; I should not like to repeat the sentences I wrote and telephoned in half an hour as they were dictated to me in Cannes by the revelation of *The 400 Blows*.

Once one has stepped back and given some thought to the film, certain defects appear. They are minor ones. The mother is less lifelike and consistent than the father. The teacher is cut from a pattern that has often been used before, and he is too much of a piece. But all the actors are excellent, and perfectly directed. Decae's photography perhaps surpasses even his highly successful *Ascenseur pour l'Echafaud* [*Frantic*] and *Le Beau Serge*. I don't know Marcel Moussy (who I am told is a remarkable television writer and director) well enough to measure his contribution (which I believe was a large one) to the scenario and the dialogue. They are both excellent. No "literary effects." A spare, fluid language, which says what is essential in simple phrases. The plot is not meant to tie the story up too neatly, as is done in certain French scenarios much influenced by a certain kind of theater, nor is there an ending full of suspense, à la Hitchcock, directed like a tournament between grand masters for the international championship. There is neither a "happy ending" nor an "unhappy ending." It's an "open end" with a question mark. It's just fine that way. Without being a mechanical and "photographic" copy, this story flows along like life.

A Review
Eric Rhode

That there's a Chaplinesque pathos about François Truffaut's *Les Quatre Cents Coups* (Curzon) isn't surprising; for like Chaplin's tramp, Antoine Doinel, the protagonist of this film, tries to live a way of life that quickly brings him into conflict with society. Antoine presents positives similar to Chaplin's: he's a bit of a dandy, full of tricks and affection, with a lovely appreciation of life, and yet a sense of its absurdity also. But for him, the conflict with society is more than a matter of pathos; for Antoine is only twelve-and-a-half years old, and his history presents in an extreme form that most tragic experience of adolescence, the loss of spontaneity. In a series of incidents of ever-increasing significance, Antoine is shown as the victim of such irresponsible people as his parents, the masters at his school, and various

From *Sight and Sound*, Spring, 1960, reprinted by permission.

social workers who have to deal with him. The more he tries to evade their tyranny, the stronger is their hold over him. The prison of his home and of his school leads to a cage at the police station, and eventually to the barred windows of an Institute for Juvenile Delinquents.

This is a deeply ironical film. For instance, Antoine's downfall is precipitated by his admiration for Balzac, one of the most eminent critics of society, and confirmed when he tries to return a stolen typewriter; and this irony takes on an increasing resonance because Antoine doesn't realize the ambiguity of social morality. At one moment, a morality picked up from films lets him down in life; at another, his parents punish him viciously for what is really a trivial offense, though they in turn are amused by the way in which a friend has fiddled his tax returns. The irony that envelops the film is truly Balzacian, involving a whole society; so that Antoine's schoolmasters and parents, especially his mother who could easily have been portrayed as a villain, are seen as victims of misunderstandings and misfortunes similar to his. And it is for this reason that Paris, which plays such a great part in this film from the credit titles onwards, is more than a stage setting. This gray Paris of dawn lights or drenched with rain (so beautifully photographed by Henri Decae) is essential to the action; and it is significant that the most moving moment in the film comes when Antoine is driven away from it in a police van. This city, which has condemned and almost destroyed him, is the place he most loves.

Truffaut has said of his film that it should be judged not by its technical perfections but by its sincerity; but of course a man's sincerity can only be judged by his technique. It is in fact through the success of his technique that Truffaut catches so much of life's richness. How can one define it? Best,

I think, by comparing it with the technique used by Alain Resnais in *Hiroshima Mon Amour;* for Resnais, in his brilliant film, uses an approach which is the most complete antithesis of Truffaut's, and in doing so brings up the most serious issue in film aesthetics. With Resnais one is always aware of art. Experiences, through subtle montage, are always wrought into aesthetic patterns so that (especially in his treatment of the bombing of Hiroshima as an allegory) one admires his wit but suspects his morality. With Truffaut, however, art conceals art; sequences are neither broken down and manipulated into aesthetic effect, nor is their moral complexity tampered with. The control of the film lies rather in the playing of complete sequences one against the other, like tesserae in a mosaic. For instance, before the tense scene in which Antoine is caught returning the typewriter, we are shown actuality shots of children absorbed in a Punch and Judy show, their faces gleaming with excitement. The point is clear—Antoine is a child like them—yet it doesn't hinder our involvement in the action. Here, as in life, we only realize the complexity of an event after we have lived through it. It follows then with complete rightness that the closing shot of this film should be ambiguous.

The camerawork shows this admirable tact also. The camera trails after Antoine as he empties his garbage can, for instance, or drinks a bottle of milk, never forcing us into an immediate judgment. The most audacious of these shots is one that already has become classical, a one-and-a-half-minute traveling shot* at the close of the film as Antoine runs away from the Institute across the countryside and down to the sea. It is clear that Truffaut has learnt much from the theories of André Bazin, to whose memory the film is dedicated.

---

* See shots 388 through 391.—*Eds.*

Bazin's belief that the film should try to capture the ambiguity and multiple levels of meaning one finds in the best novels is amply carried out here: but always in terms of the immediate, of the subtle, significant detail. With the most delicate of touches Truffaut builds up a picture of Antoine's home, of its disorder and his neglect; or, more amusingly, the bizarre home of René, Antoine's friend, with its stuffed horse and its multitude of fat, purring cats. Relationships are caught in a simple, startling action; Antoine's affection for his mother is shown briefly in the fond way he handles the perfume and brushes on her dressing-table. But Truffaut's most impressive accomplishment is to catch the improvised quality of life; and this, one suspects, is why he is so much at home with children. The scenes in the classroom are both tender and funny; without knowing it, one boy systematically messes up an entire exercise book, while another one only finds inspiration for his essay as the master tells the boys to stop writing. And it is because of this talent for improvisation that Truffaut manages to bring out such a magnificent performance from his Antoine (Jean-Pierre Léaud), of whom Truffaut has said: "I encouraged him to play by ear. He performed freely, reacting in his own manner and responding in his own words." The success of this method is most apparent in the weakest part of the excellent script (by Truffaut and Marcel Moussy), when Antoine is questioned by the analyst at the Institute. In fact the boy's naturalness and charm, and Truffaut's lightness of direction, make this scene wholly successful; and it is finally, indeed, through Truffaut's lightness of touch and zest for life, and through Léaud's realization of Antoine's stoicism and almost cockney resilience, that this film never becomes portentous or depressing. It is, truly, a film that speaks up for life.

How New? How Vague?
Norman N. Holland

A similar but far less successful step toward truth
and away from goodness [than Louis Malle's *The
Lovers*] is taken by François Truffaut's *The 400
Blows*, which took the Best Direction Prize at
Cannes . . . Truffaut has announced he wanted to
make a film about a child without any of the usual
prettification for the coos of the menopause set. In
that he has succeeded, but unfortunately he has paid
the price of significance for it. His film details the
miseries of a twelve- or thirteen-year-old boy, mis-
understood by his promiscuous mother and his easy-
going *cocu* of a father. In sharp contrast with these
tiresome realities are the silly fakeries of the world
imposed on the child by the adult establishment,
notably the tyrannical school. Contrasted to the cheery
fantasies of the movies (Truffaut puts in a plug for
his friend Rivette's *Paris Nous Appartient*) or a children's puppet show (some of the best shots in the
film are of children spellbound by the puppets),
the school feeds the children dear little fables which
seem, somehow, no longer to apply. In a sense you
could sum up the discrepancy between the false
world imposed on the child and the real world of
adults by the progression from the impossible post-
office pen the boy must use in school to the fountain
pen he really uses to the typewriter he steals and for
which his parents send him off to reform school.

The one recurring image of the film is escape: all
the characters break out of the limits imposed on
them by society and pretty much get away with it.
The father has his sportscars, the mother her affairs;

From *The Hudson Review*, Vol. XIII, No. 2 (Summer,
1960). Copyright © 1960 by The Hudson Review, Inc.
Reprinted by permission.

both are efforts to break out of their tiny, cramped apartment. The boy's chum successfully plays truant and in an hilarious sequence we see the escape one-by-one of a class being marched out to compulsory athletics, again, getting away with it as the hero seems never able to. Balanced against these efforts to escape are the classrooms, the queues, the locks and bars of prisons, all the *apparat* of social confinement. The boy suffers the ultimate confinement and escape: he runs away from the reform school and rushes to the sea he has always wanted to look upon. Yet, this, too, seems an edge, the final confinement, and he turns away from the sea to stare shoreward and enigmatically into the camera. In this last of a long series of regressions from city to country to primeval amniotic sea, the picture turns into a still as though the camera itself had given up motion. Truffaut's film has many virtues, but in the last analysis, it lapses into a mere case history, not a work of art. In the reform school the tone is shattered by a tactless interview with a psychiatrist straight out of the worst kind of social-worker documentary and far too often, throughout the film, irrelevant episodes take over and warp its logical growth. Perhaps because the story is autobiographical, Truffaut seems unable to give his realistic material any shaping and form; he seems to have reached an extreme of vagueness that even *la nouvelle vague* can scarcely tolerate.

A Review
Arlene Croce

François Truffaut's first feature, *The 400 Blows*, is one of the few masterpieces of its kind granted to the cinema in recent years. It is a sad, bitter story of a child's gradual disaffection from society. The child is tough, imaginative, exuberant; the society is dull, timid, corrupt. And the film's point of view isn't sentimental. Antoine, the hero (in a jewel of a performance by Jean-Pierre Léaud), is a completely spontaneous and engaging extrovert of thirteen or fourteen, neither more nor less remarkable or sensitive than his classmates. He doesn't breach the pattern in any way. He does, however, get caught. For showing a certain mild defiance, he gets a reputation as a trouble-maker, and petty-bourgeois vindictiveness does the rest. Forced out of school, betrayed by parents for whom he represents the burden of an impossible marriage, he is consigned to the police and the vice-ridden world of adults. The "good-bye to all that" gesture of the finale has some of the proud fantasy of Lamorisse's films—the suggestion that freedom lies not in the present world of corruption but in another time and place, the time and place that a child conceives of in his imagination, where he is in his element. In a recent interview in *The New Yorker*, Truffaut dismissed the white manes and red balloons as sentimental and irrelevant additives to the child's world. But because he makes his own kind of poetry, and because he takes the path of realism, he is in no danger of being confused with Lamorisse. Unlike the Lamorisse films, *The 400 Blows* does not exist on a plane of fantasy; its prem-

Reprinted from *Film Quarterly*, Vol. XIII, No. 3 (Spring, 1960) pp. 35–38, by permission of The Regents. Copyright © 1960 by The Regents of the University of California.

ises are not allegorical. It is about the suffering an average young schoolboy must endure if he has the bad luck to be considered a criminal by both his family and the state in what we can only take to be present-day Paris. Given the actualities of this situation, and a manifest talent for observation, Truffaut's approach may seem to American audiences strangely stoical. He seems to be able to accept bad luck in good grace and still move us to moral indignation.

Truffaut is not, in the political sense, engaged. He protests in terms of the transcendent values; he protests the inhumanity of man. The underlying sadness of this film is the sadness of the universal estrangement. Truffaut's beautifully oblique style of commentary is a product of poetic intuition, not, I dare say, of political evasion. In *The 400 Blows*, "new wave" technique serves to unite poetry and journalism in the powerful idiom of a particular environment—an environment, moreover, that has long supplied certain historical privileges for what an aesthetic need can make of them. On its most agreeable level, you see something of this environmental idiom in the style of an Yves Montand, and you see the difference between that and what one critic has called "the desperate strategies" of our own popular entertainers. An American filmmaker who wished to present with sympathy and truth the predicament of the young Antoines of New York and Detroit would really have to *faire les quatre cents coups*—and risk bad art as well as public indifference. What Truffaut has achieved—a genuinely un-neurotic work of public art—is something that seems at present quite beyond the capacity of American filmmakers to produce, and not only because of Hollywood. Our own tradition provides no model, no cultural precedent for the kind of radical humanism we need today—unless it be the image of Huck Finn lighting out for that territory. The image is apolitical because the society that produced it was practically nonindustrial. To an incomparably greater degree than in the days of Mark Twain, however, politics is the way we live. You don't find many valid images of revolt today. An omnivorous society swallows the more fashionable ones whole, and the others are all bound in the pages of *Dissent* magazine. Truffaut's hero also lights out. He might be the hero of a film made thirty years ago. We Americans don't live in the past, as Richard Nixon says. We most emphatically don't. The violent flux of American life constantly revises the artist's scale of reference. Whereas even the rebellion of Holden Caulfield begins to seem like an inner-directed archaism when compared to the enormities of present-day teen-age culture, the children of *The 400 Blows* seem to be growing up in a relatively unaltered social surround. Whether or not this is part of the provincialism Truffaut is attacking, it does give the film a perennial truth, an air of timelessness, and I think the obvious allusions to *Zéro de Conduite* help to point this out.

The 400 Blows is a film about freedom. It could, I think, convey this idea to an audience of deaf illiterates in any part of the world, because its construction is very nearly as absolutely visual as that of a silent film. Its metaphor for freedom is space, as in that other great escape film, *Grand Illusion*. Notice the deceptively casual way both films gradually broaden in scope, in both the dramatic and the optical sense. To take *The 400 Blows*: who would have thought its end was in its beginning? It opens with crowded shots of a decrepit classroom packed with Vigo's grubby scholars under the tyrannical eye of a master half-demented through exhaustion; later come perambulations in and around Montmartre, a maze of architectural restrictions, reflecting a life so cramped, limited, and circular that the hero, playing hooky one day, spots his mother in *flagrante delicto;* and the wedged-in life of the tenements . . . Against all these things, Truffaut presses an unsparing camera. But the mood is relaxed, footling, the film moves at an even speed. We seem to be watching trivia, amusing and somewhat inconsequential. The musical score, with its jogging tunes, seems to reinforce this impression. The scene in the revolving drum injects the first disturbing note. It is, perhaps, a presentiment of brutalization. A small, blurred figure flattened on the side of an enormous whirling cylinder, and the cylinder turning in the expanse of the widescreen—for a moment the film itself seems to be out of control. But Truffaut passes lightly over it, and things resume their old prosaic proportions. Except that now the isolation of the boy creates a new series of involvements, to which Truffaut responds with a subtle increase in momentum and an instinct for incongruities that move the film decisively out of the range of anecdote onto a level of profoundly serious narrative. By the time the boy's father hands him over to the police with all the callous piety that seems necessary to the occasion, the transition in tone is complete: this is no joke. The scenes of incarceration which follow pull you way under. The boy is flung into a cage with some routine offenders and then into a smaller one, the size of a phone booth, by himself. It is only the first of the many times we are to see children behind bars before the film comes to its close, with a great climactic letting-in of air.

The most original feature of Truffaut's beautifully oblique style of commentary is his by-now famous use of protracted sequences accomplished through the sustained single shot and through a minimum of cutting: the scene in the revolving drum [shots 74–93]; the long ride in the paddy wagon which encompasses the boy's whole descent from innocence, and which I recall as one long close-up alternated with a single reverse-field shot [shots 318–325]; the extraordinary interview with the (off-screen) psychiatrist, in which there are no cuts, merely a series of unsettling dissolves [shots 358–363]; and the long tracking shot of the stupendous finale [shot 390]. Since cutting is a director's chief means of comment, the effects Truffaut obtains in these sequences depend on the progression of meanings within the frame. Sometimes, as in the examples cited above, the progression has the elliptical motion of fine poetry. At other times, there is little more than the amateur perpetuation of a cliché. The physical-culture outing, for all its obvious debt to Vigo, looks like nothing so much as tired Tati (which is pretty tired), and the puppet show episode is sheer *tourisme*.

Where there is poetry in Truffaut's method, it is often graced with the kind of ambiguity cherished among the "new wave" directors. The ambiguity derives from a deliberate withholding of explicit comment, as in the interview scene—from the apparent determination of the director to express no opinions. Revelation is a matter of the direct perception of what people say and do, and what is revealed to you is your own feeling about the words and deeds of others. For example, shortly after the boy's commitment to the reformatory, a judge is seen wearily assuring the boy's mother that he will do what he can. In opposition to this paternal image, which might almost be out of some government-sponsored information film, we later see a semi-conscious young runaway being dragged back to captivity. The grown-up characters in the film may appear to us monsters of hypocrisy, but is it more correct to say that they control the world than to say that they are controlled by it? In either case, children suffer. Instead of a moral pattern in the conventional sense, you are confronted with the spectacle of unanalyzed phenomena. Conventionally speaking, the boy's father is an ami-

254

able coward, his mother a hard-shelled Bovary ("I'm used to being criticized!")—the nearest thing to a villain in the piece. But no one can say they don't "try." Similarly, the judge, the psychiatrist, the chief of police all do their best, they "have children of their own." But, as we soon see, the caretaker locks his three little girls in a pen when the boys come running out for sports, and the runaway, accepting smuggled food, declares he would do it all again for just five more days of freedom. If Antoine judges his world, he does so through the only means that are available to him—a pure-hearted instinct for decency that, in the end, makes him take to his heels. Away he goes in a cross-country run that seems to take him clear across France to the sea. In the surf, liberated at last, he turns momentarily to face us; the image freezes, then slowly it fades out.

In its retention of life's ambiguity, the "new wave" technique makes unique demands on the spectator. The novelty of it is the way it can open up a film in the mind of the audience, creating an experience which is insistently problematical. This is perhaps more true of Chabrol than it is of Truffaut, but even when Truffaut seems to be putting things squarely up to you, as in the intense and disarming intimacy of the psychiatrist's interview, ambiguous sensations are evident, and there is a suspicion that, in some of the things he says, the boy may be lying. As he himself remarks, "When I tell the truth, they don't believe me." The important thing, however, is that at this moment, and at the end, you are no longer looking at the film—the film is looking at you. In Franju's words (*Cahiers du Cinéma*): "*Il parle au public, le môme, il nous parle.*" What a blessing.